SIMPLE MATTERS

SIMPLE MATTERS

ERIN BOYLE

Living with Less and
Ending Up with More

ABRAMS IMAGE
NEW YORK

CONTENTS

Introduction: Making a Home   06

01: Decluttering   12
02: Simplifying   40
03: Organizing   72
04: Decorating   90
05: Bath & Beauty   112
06: Getting Dressed   126
07: Cooking & Entertaining   140
08: Cleaning   156
09: Thriving   170

Notes   188
Acknowledgments   191

Introduction: Making a Home

"Tis a gift to be simple, 'tis a gift to be free, 'tis a gift to come down where you ought to be."
—Shaker dance song by Joseph Brackett

Many minimalist narratives begin with too much. Too much disposable income, too many unnecessary purchases, too much stuff—and not enough happiness. This isn't one of those narratives.

My story begins in an echoey old apartment in downtown Wilmington, North Carolina. It begins in a kitchen that came complete with too-tall-by-far wooden cabinets coated in ten layers of paint, pitted Formica countertops, and palmetto bugs (translation: cockroaches, southern-style) that skittered in twenty different directions as soon as the lights flickered on. There were more palmetto bugs than there was anything else.

I was a few days past twenty-three. James was a few months past twenty-five. A year and a half later, I would write my first blog post. Eventually we'd leave North Carolina for Providence, Rhode Island, where I'd go to graduate school and James would finish his master's thesis. We'd move together into a tiny apartment in Brooklyn. I'd begin to write about life in that place. After a year there, we'd get married. We'd have a baby—and need to move again. But before all that, there was our beginning. Our beginning, in our first apartment.

I arrived to that apartment for the first time after dark.

James had found it several weeks before, while I was living abroad. Ours had been a long-distance relationship, our time together limited—and made richer—by our experiences in far-flung places. On dusky, chardonnay-scented bicycle rides through the vineyards of southern Burgundy, I'd made up my mind to join James in North Carolina once the school year ended. He'd be starting a graduate program, I'd be re-acclimating to life in the U.S. and searching for work.

James sent me pictures of the apartment he'd found for us to live in. He knew what to highlight. The fireplace and the bay windows and the porch with a swing. There weren't any pictures of the palmetto bugs.

We exchanged emails about what we'd do to fix broken screens and hide a gas heater that took up half of the living room. We didn't yet know about the transient man with a penchant for poking his head through the bay window. Or the neighbor who would, one night, build a raging bonfire in the ten-foot space between our two tinderbox Queen Anne houses. We didn't know about the bathroom ceiling that would eventually collapse during our tenure, or the stove that we'd come to learn leaked carbon monoxide. When we arrived, we only knew we had to make it our own.

And so, more-or-less fresh off the plane from a year of teaching elementary school in France, I found a mattress and a box spring in the bedroom made up with clean, ecru-colored sheets. James had bought them himself, sprawling on mattress after mattress until he found one that he thought would suit us both. There was a couch that he'd begged off a couple moving their young family cross-country. There was a washer and dryer that he'd hustled into our back room via a hastily rented U-Haul. In the kitchen: two saucepans.

Two summers before, James had spent the summer on Edisto Island, South Carolina. The local Piggly Wiggly had been running a promotion with Royal Doulton, and he'd saved up the points he accumulated with each receipt and purchased the stainless-steel pans. He'd been toting them around as he went from seasonal work contract to seasonal work contract— crisscrossing the country while chasing sea turtle research projects and ski slopes.

We were adults—or so we'd told our parents. We tried to prove it to ourselves, the best way that we could, as we made a life together in a state hundreds of miles from the places where we'd grown up. Because adults had homes. And homes were more than just four walls and a bed. And so I unzipped my suitcases and hung a few dresses in the closet. Somewhere a palmetto bug skittered across the floor.

Making a home is hard work, and for some reason it's underappreciated. It's a way to make sense of things. As we figured out how to pay for our rent, we also spent hours talking about dishes, about how to sweep scattered insect carcasses properly out the banging screen door. We lay in bed and day-dreamed about what curtains to hang.

On lonely afternoons after work, I would prowl around antique shops looking for a chair or a table lamp or a mirror that would make our place *feel* like a home. In the hours when I wasn't working, I busied myself with projects: removing the broken, ill-fitting shades in each window and hanging up curtains instead—gauzy ones, bought cheaply and hung just one to each window to save on the cost.

We bought a mop, and James scrubbed our hardwood floors. He did it over and over and over again until we could walk on them without our bare feet sticking with each step. Even after the last wash, the mop water still turned gray.

In our first week together, I spent precious pennies on a new blue-and-white-striped cloth shower curtain. I hung up the curtain and then decided that the tub looked dingy by comparison. Bleach, I reasoned, would do the trick. While I sprayed at the ancient layer of grime in the tub, an accidental stream hit the cloth curtain, which became specked with orange before my eyes. I slumped myself onto the dirty bathroom floor in defeat. It was only a shower curtain. And yet it had come to signify a lot more: an attempt to be grown-up. A stab at making a grungy place feel like home. A triumph of penny-pinching. I called my mom and I cried.

James left me empty beer bottles filled with flowers on the kitchen windowsill. We began untangling the brambles in the front garden. We propped surfboards in corners for safekeeping and . . . decor. We bought terracotta pots and filled them with ivy. We hung our clothes in the narrow shared closet. We hauled home, cleaned, and rejected a series of shabby dressers until we settled on a pair to sand and paint and love. I bought a quilt that cost as much as my weekly paycheck, which is to say, not much.

There were seemingly endless decisions to make and more choices than we could have imagined. We needed a mop, but which mop? We needed soap, but which soap? Flour: white or wheat? Napkins: cloth or paper? Detergent: liquid or powder? I remember retail paralysis under the unflattering fluorescent lights of store after store.

But it wasn't just about the *stuff*. Everything we did in that space felt imbued with meaning. *Are you really going to hang that, there? You fold your underwear how?* And we were learning. We were deciding what habits we'd borrow from our parents and which we'd reject. We were learning what habits we would borrow from each other. And what we would cut from whole cloth for ourselves. There wasn't anyone telling us what to do, but at the same time it felt as if everyone was telling us what to do: a lifetime of often-contradictory advice about what was nice to have and what was essential to have.

James grumbled about tofu, and I turned my nose up at steak. Hungrily, we worked out what we would make for dinner. We both loved eating by candlelight. We bought candles and put them in the center of our table and we lit them. It didn't matter if it was our third night in a row eating pasta; we lit candles every night.

There were missteps. Things collected that we didn't really need. Money spent that might have been saved. Arguments that we'd one day learn to navigate.

And what we learned in that first apartment we carried with us to our second one. We settled on a brand of soap. We bought flour and a jar to keep it in. We made choices about cable and Internet and electricity and gas. We learned how to shop at the farmers' market. We found a local grocery store. We took long rides to the beach. We tried to give each other space to breathe. Sometimes we didn't, and we learned from that, too.

By the time James and I moved into our tiny apartment in Brooklyn, we'd been living together for four years in as many apartments. Four apartments that we'd moved into, unpacked, tried to make our own.

In that little space, with a footprint of just 173 square feet, I realized that our resilient sanity in such tight quarters was because of choices that we'd *already* made. There was plenty that we had to part with. Baskets and books and furniture that didn't make the cut. But moving into that tiny apartment didn't change our lifestyle as much as it brought it into sharper focus.

We'd never lived in such a tiny space, but we had learned a thing or two about resourcefulness. We'd developed an understanding that the first step is to push open the windows. And the second step is scrubbing the place clean. And the third step is making the bed and maybe arranging a bouquet of flowers and taking a deep breath or two.

My hope for this book is that it does similar work. That in telling some of my stories and in sharing some of what's worked in the places where I've lived, I can offer simple solutions to inspire a similar kind of fresh air. A metaphorical opening of the windows and scrubbing of the floors.

Lives are complicated. In the same years that we were learning to make our home, we endured other deeply human experiences. We experienced death and crime and sudden grief. We continued falling in love. We missed our families. We wrung our hands about our careers. We plotted our futures. In some moments, we felt unspeakable joy. And we found that life isn't always simple. But the curtains can be.

That's what this book is about. The simple decisions and practices and objects and habits that make up the backdrop of our tumultuous lives. It's a book about the pleasure of simple materials and honest design and the advantage of slowing down. It offers approaches to making a home that are gentler on the planet, but also gentler on ourselves, on our bank accounts, on our sense of self. It's a book based on the premise that a simple home is filled with hardworking things. It acknowledges that as we design our homes, we must be stewards of the world beyond our private sphere.

More than an aesthetic or economic choice, living simply requires conscious acts. By consuming less, purchasing more thoughtfully, and sending fewer things to the landfill, we can free up time and space for the things that really matter. By making useful art out of any square footage, we can improve the tenor of our days. No matter who or where you are, you can make your life matter, simply.

01:

Decluttering

01:   Decluttering

"Less, but better."
—Dieter Rams

The June day when James and I moved into our tiny Brooklyn apartment was hot. Not stifling hot, but hot enough to let us know that spring was out and summer was arriving. James and I had packed up our apartment in Providence the day before with the help of my mom and dad. We'd already done the work of selling off what we knew wouldn't fit into our new place: a futon we'd been hoping to part ways with anyway, two desks that we'd made from a length of thick birch plywood, a chifforobe that had been one of our favorite Craigslist finds to date but that we knew we'd never be able to squeeze into our new place. Our furniture went to friends mostly—other graduate students who were staying on in Providence. There were boxes of books that we packed knowing we'd be able to slide them into the attic at my mom and dad's house. There was an antique headboard that would go in an outdoor shed in their yard, too tall to clear the ceiling of the loft where we'd be sleeping.

As we packed the moving van, we were confident. We'd done this together before. We knew how to arrange the boxes so they'd fit into the truck just right. We'd stop at my parents' house in Connecticut and unload our books and headboard, and then we'd be on our way. It would be an easy move. But as the truck filled up, I felt a tightening in my chest. It was hard to imagine exactly what the apartment had looked like a few weeks earlier when we'd signed our lease. And now, standing in front of the open moving van, I was sure that we still had too much. The contents of a home undressed from closets and cabinets and dresser drawers make for an overwhelming tower, even for someone who's discerning about accumulation.

When we pulled in front of our new building on that hot June day, we left our truck double-parked in the street and flipped the flashers on. Before unpacking a single thing, we went inside to see our apartment for the second time.

I wish I could write that upon opening the door we breathed a sigh of relief. But the truth is that we laughed and took a sharp breath. Emptied of all of the previous tenant's belongings, bafflingly, the shoebox of a room appeared even smaller than it had when filled. The apartment looked like a hallway—a place that could only reasonably lead somewhere else. And of course, I'm fairly sure that it *was* part of a former hallway—a tiny apartment squeezed into what had formerly been the end of a ten-foot-wide great hall. It was a ridiculous little space, but it was ours and we had a truck to unpack.

Our breathing came easier with the unpacking. Our clothes went back into dresser drawers. Our ornery but still kind building superintendent helped us lift one dresser into our loft, where against all odds we also managed to fit our bed. Our cups and plates and bowls got unwrapped from newspaper and arranged in cabinets. There was a closet—albeit a tiny one—for stashing still more. By the time we were finished unpacking, the place actually looked spare. The pile of boxes had disappeared. We'd managed to only bring what we needed.

You don't need to have lived a life of excess or be moving into a tiny apartment to realize that you have more than you need. But stemming the tide of *stuff* that enters a home can be a challenge even for a self-proclaimed minimalist.

The good news: decluttering doesn't have to mean getting rid of everything that you own and starting over. You can move into a tiny apartment, but you can also stay precisely where you are and make a decision to live lightly.

The first step? Cut the existing fat.

More begets more. It stands in the face of reason, but when we have too much stuff we're likely to amass still more of it. We

forget what we have. We start looking for solutions to contain
what is already there, and in the process we bury what we started
with and add to our ever-growing pile. We end up overwhelmed.

A relationship with material objects is not inherently bad.
But our homes are too often cluttered with things that we don't
really need—or worse, things we don't like much at all. In a
world where with the click of a few buttons and the stroke of
even fewer keys we can have at our doorsteps any number
of conveniences, we buy too much, keep too much, equate stuff
with happiness and happiness with stuff, and lose ourselves
somewhere along the way. And this skewed relationship can
make us feel very bad indeed.

In the early 2000s, a team of researchers at UCLA under-
took a study the likes of which had never been done before.
They conducted anthropological research on thirty-two families
in Los Angeles as a way to gain a bit of insight into how the
modern American family functions. Their study acknowledges
that at the time, the United States was "the most materially
rich society in global history."[1] The result is homes filled to
brimming with material possessions. As part of the study,
trained coders counted material objects in subjects' homes.
In the first household, an incredible 2,260 *visible* possessions
were noted in the living room and two bedrooms alone. That's
not counting what lay hidden in closets or dresser drawers
or tucked behind another object.[2] More than being crowded,
researchers reported that "the visual busyness of hoards of
objects can affect basic enjoyment of the home." Study partici-
pants who identified their homes as being messy and cluttered
experienced a higher rate of depressed moods in the evening
based on cortisol measures taken over a series of days."[3]

And then there's this: The average American family has
2,598 square feet of living space.[4] Into that space gets crammed
an enormous quantity of consumer goods. In 2009, the U.S.
Bureau of Labor Statistics reported that Americans collectively
spent $1.13 trillion on discretionary purchases alone. What
doesn't fit within our homes, Americans are casting off to

self-storage units. According to the industry's lobbying organization (the Self Storage Association, naturally), the industry generated more than $24 billion in annual revenues in the United States in 2013 and boasts 2.3 billion square feet of rentable space.

Life is messy, sure. But *2.3 billion square feet?* Ask me, and I think this smacks of a mess that's grown out of control. And there's an element of the mess that I think we can control before it controls us.

Decluttering means looking carefully at what you have and making decisions about what you should keep, and then taking steps to eliminate the rest. The result is not only a home that feels clean and fresh, but one that brings you comfort and a sense of peace.

When we make a commitment to using our purchasing power wisely, we set off a chain reaction that affects people we've never met and places we've never been for the better. In the end, decluttering isn't only about the order it brings to our messy lives. It's about the implications it will eventually have outside of them, too.

Getting Started

This is where we begin: Get rid of anything that isn't doing work. The things in our homes should earn their keep. They should do the work of being beautiful, or bringing us joy, or helping us out in our daily lives. Anything that isn't doing work is simply taking up space. And in my home—and I'd guess in yours too—space is sacred.

Getting rid of something doesn't mean sweeping it under the proverbial rug, or relocating it to storage, or coaxing someone else to shoulder the burden until you've made a long-term decision. It's about tackling the tough questions now. It means being stoic in the face of sentimentality; it means not looking back once you've decided that something should go. This is the hard part, but it's also the easy part.

A clutter-free kitchen table means having a space that's ready for work, whether that's the work of serving dinner, or hosting a cup of tea with a friend, or serving as a toddler's art station.

I got my first taste of clearing out the clutter in middle school. I had a desk in my bedroom as a child that I rarely sat at but that I dutifully filled with treasures. There was a motley collection of bouncy balls. Miscellaneous rocks from trips to the beach. Paper clips that I'd deemed *fancy* and worth stashing. And on and on. Those trolls with stick-up hair and jeweled belly buttons? I had a few. Those triangular pencil grips meant to teach perfect pencil-grasping? Three or four of those. Scrunchies? Oh, yes.

On one weekend morning, my mom gave me a large Tupperware container and told me to clear out the desk and fill the container only with the things that I would still want to have when I was sixty. Faced with many drawers of keepsakes and only one box, it was clear that I would need to reassess the value of those paper clips and ordinary beach stones. I deposited the beach stones into my mom's garden path and amassed an enormous pile of plastic trinkets to give away. The result was a collection of considered keepsakes, desk drawers that could open and close, and the giddy feeling of a fresh start.

To help get your head around what you might relieve yourself of, I think it's helpful to put the extraneous into three categories: trash, redundancies, and unnecessaries.

Trash

Let's start with trash. Even though we might let it pile up, when tasked to get rid of trash we can easily identify it, and few heartstrings are tugged when we wrangle a pile of old catalogs or junk mail.

For lots of people, keeping clutter in the form of trash at bay comes down to being a matter of habit. Consider checking the mail. Most days, I check my mail at the mailbox and throw anything that I don't need to keep directly into the recycling bins outside our building. If there's a catalog I want to look at, I might bring that upstairs. But if I haven't flipped through it by the end of the day, it goes into the straw basket I keep by the apartment door for corralling recyclables. If there is something that I need to address, I'll usually tackle it within a few minutes of bringing it inside. If I don't tend to the mail right away, it has the tendency to get lost in the shuffle and then forgotten. Sometimes I recycle something before James has had a chance to page through it. But I never have piles.

Maybe obvious trash isn't your problem.

Slightly more work might be required to convince yourself to finally ditch tattered and worn clothing, half-empty paint cans and shampoo bottles, or singleton socks and earrings. You might feel stymied by the impulse that says that these things might still be *useful*. A tattered shirt can serve as a uniform for mowing the lawn. The half-empty shampoo bottle might be refilled later. The missing earring might still turn up. But despite this mental chatter, the overwhelming likelihood is that they *won't* be useful. You likely have more shirts relegated to the "for gardening only" pile than ones you can wear to work. You've probably condemned that half-empty shampoo bottle to go unused the moment you open a new one. Chances are that your missing earring is down a subway grate, never to be seen again. Rather than being an admonishment, this realization can be freeing. Let these things go—they're gone already.

An exercise might be useful here: Imagine the current state of your medicine cabinet. If its shelves are sparsely lined with only items that you use on a regular basis, then you are off to a terrific start. But if you imagine it and see shelves lined with half-used lotions, glittery makeup samples you'd never wear out of the house, empty contact cases, and expired prescriptions, you'll understand what I mean by trash. A bathroom cabinet is a small and contained space designed for holding *necessary* things that we use on a daily basis. But even in that confined area, the tendency is to leave the clutter well enough alone—to shut the door and forget the mess until the next day. And too quickly, the next day becomes the next and the detritus goes untackled. The best strategy for these spaces is the clean-slate approach.

Take a garbage bag into the bathroom, open your cabinet, and remove every single thing that you know without a shadow of a doubt that you will never use again: the deodorant you bought that didn't work, the lotion that made you break out, the dried-up mascara, the razor blades that fit a long-since-lost handle. Once those are gone, take another look at the cabinet and remove everything that you only use rarely: the false eyelashes, the blue mascara, the orange lipstick. Think for a minute about the last time you used those things. If it was longer than a year ago, consider the shelf life of cosmetics (hint: it's not long) and toss them. Then think about how happy a clutter-free space might make you feel. At the end of the exercise, you should have a bathroom cabinet that looks like something out of a catalog. We'll talk specifics about the things you might put back in later on, but for now rest easy knowing that you've cleared your slate.

Breathing easier? Let's continue.

We keep our bathroom cabinet reserved for essentials like toothpaste. I keep all of my makeup in a travel toiletry case. I like this solution because it keeps my collection down to the essentials, and it means I'm always packed and ready to go.

The trash category also contains more-difficult-to-throw-away items whose useful life is still nonetheless over: outdated electronics, busted toys, damaged luggage. While it's easy to identify these things as unuseful, they require a bit more effort to get rid of. I'm calling these things trash not because I'm suggesting that they should end up in a landfill. Many of them can and should be recycled (we'll get to that), but the alternative to throwing them away shouldn't be allowing them to hole up in your house.

I am guilty of this myself. When the first laptop that I bought after college finally conked out, I held onto it. I packed it into a moving van (twice!). I wanted to get rid of it responsibly, but I felt daunted by researching what that method was. And to dive into the psyche just a little bit more: Part of me didn't want to get rid of something that I had worked so hard to buy in the first place. And yet, it wasn't serving a single, solitary purpose in my home. These are the kinds of things that have to go. *See the donation guidelines on page 36.*

Redundancies

Once the actual trash is cleared, tackle the redundancies: those things that replicate what you already own. The kitchen appliance that does nearly the same thing as another. The extra sweatshirts, the second set of mixing bowls, the fourth cast-iron pan, the seventh pair of black tights. The winter jacket you can only wear on days when the mercury dips below freezing but you happen to live in a climate where that never happens. You get my point.

Like so many good Girl Scouts or Boy Scouts, we too often approach our homes with the attitude of *Always Prepared*, when the better approach might be *Prepared Enough*. The irony is most of us likely live within close proximity to the things we'd want to have should the need suddenly arise. And yet, we Americans tend to stockpile. Just because the dentist offers you another set of clean toothbrushes doesn't mean you have to take them. Storing ten new toothbrushes so that you can have them on hand in the unlikely event that ten houseguests have forgotten their own means being able to heroically hand out a free tooth-brush once in a blue moon and living with clutter the rest of the time. There are people who will disagree with me on this point. They will say that they prefer to be prepared, that they want an extra set of sheets and clean toothbrushes and a loaner jacket to give a visitor who arrives on a rainy day. These are noble wishes. But they are not wishes that allow you to live with less.

So here's what I suggest: Pull open your drawers, swing open your closets, and go on a treasure hunt for all of those things that you have more than one of. Then pare down to just one.

Let's take throw blankets as an example. When James and I moved into our first apartment together, he brought with him not one but two throw blankets sewn from thick cotton fleece of the variety used to make college sweatshirts. These blankets took the sweatshirt look-alike contest a step further and bore the insignia of actual universities (along with a few suspicious grease stains). Added together with the throw blankets that I had—which included a pilly cotton blanket I'd used in my own college dorm room—we had four blankets, none of which we especially loved. We could have thrown them into a large basket to save for just-in-case, but we decided to look at the pile and ask ourselves which blankets we liked *best*. It was the time for superlatives. And gut checks. We ditched the sweatshirt blankets that seemed better suited to tailgating than snuggling on the couch. We gave away my irreparably pilly blanket, and we committed to using the fourth until we'd saved enough to purchase a simple blanket that matched the rest of our space. This is my best advice for gaining control over your stuff: Take deliberate action. If there are extra throw blankets lurking in a basket by your couch, do yourself and your home a favor and simply get rid of them.

Unnecessaries   These are items you neither love nor need but that manage to stay around. These items are gifts, or once-precious things that you worked hard for or once loved, but are patently not useful. Among the list: plastic soccer trophies from grade school, miscellany that might loosely fall into the dangerous category of decor, tote bags emblazoned with the name of a conference you went to a lifetime ago, textbooks from college, *notes* from textbooks from college.

The thing to remember is that not everything that once served a purpose, or marked an occasion, remains forever useful.

Take the example of college notes. Your notebook might be filled with neatly drawn equations that are a testament to your ability to conquer calculus. (I imagine. There has never been such a notebook in my life.) You wonder if maybe one day you will go back to school and if those notes will be useful. Chances are slim on both counts.

There are always exceptions to the rule. In the year after I graduated from college, I taught English in France. I hand-drew worksheets and flashcards and other teaching tools to use with my students. I labored over them. I almost threw them out one summer in a fit of decluttering, but then my sister made me pause. "You can use these to teach your kids French one day," she said. (And if anything, she's more unflinching than I in tossing things out.) But she was right: They're not *essential*, but they're definitely useful. And a tad sentimental. And so I have kept them. I have not kept every paper I wrote in college. I have not kept every birthday card I have ever received. I've made choices, and so should you. More has to go than has to stay, but not *everything* has to go.

Beyond the emotionally fraught world of the once-useful, there's the emotionally fraught world of the things that were never useful. The decorative salt shaker from your great aunt? The one in the shape of bunnies meant to serve you in the two weeks of the year that flank Easter? The ones you don't even *like*. Free yourself of the burden. The wedding favor bearing the name of the bride and groom? You might love the bride and groom, but that doesn't mean you need a mug with their names on it. *Let it go*.

We're under the false impression that we're not in control of our spaces, when the opposite is true. I understand that the specifics of what you feel that you can or cannot give up are complex, but remember that everything in your home is taking up precious room. Breathing room. *Living room.* And most of these things? You will simply not miss them once they're gone.

The things you love are the things you'll keep. Reconsider everything else.

My childhood desk is proof that I don't exactly have an inborn tendency toward minimalism. But if I was pressed to identify a consistent factor in my choice as an adult to live with less, frequent moving—even more than the relatively small size of my apartments—has been most important.

Every few months I assess my closet and drawers and get rid of anything that no longer fits, has torn beyond repair, or that I've simply realized I don't wear often enough to justify it taking up space in my drawers.

I have a small photo box where I keep a collection of special photographs, along with a copy of my wedding invitation and a handful of special letters.

Choosing which throw blanket to love is a question of personal taste, but I love that a simple white blanket always looks neat and clean—even when it's tossed unceremoniously on a couch or bed.

In the past ten years, I've lived in five different apartments. I've moved to new apartments across state lines, and on two separate occasions, to a new apartment less than two blocks away from my old one. But the distance between the apartments hasn't mattered. Wrapped up in paper, carefully layered into boxes, taped, labeled, moved up and down stairs and unpacked again, my possessions have been literal weights to carry. Each time I've moved, I've had the opportunity to take stock. In asking myself if I would want to move something, I've come to identify the things that I truly love and the things that are truly useful. I've naturally prioritized my things. And in the end, I've given away what I haven't wanted, donated or sold what I'll never use again, and reorganized everything that I've been left with.

Even if frequent moving is not something that you're inclined toward, you can practice the same kind of assessment. Every few years, approach every corner of your home with the question of whether you'd take the things in it with you if it meant physically moving them somewhere new. Chances are, you'd be willing to move less than you're willing to store.

Gatekeeping

Congrats on decluttering so far, but the road to cleared-out spaces doesn't end there. The bigger problem than getting rid of things is the problem of acquiring them in the first place.

In addition to divesting yourself of stuff, commit to barring from entry anything that is not useful or lovely or hopefully both.

To commit to maintaining your clutter-free home, you'll likely need to make a few broadstroke changes to your relationship with stuff and its place in the space where you live. If you have a personal (therapeutic of course!) shopping habit, you'll probably need to restrict it (or put it to use for a family in need). You might encourage friends and family to help you in your new endeavor. Instead of filling a wedding registry with every kitchen gadget you can find in a store's catalog, consider having guests contribute to a travel fund. Instead of creating a detailed baby registry, think about asking guests to contribute to a single big-ticket item like a stroller or carseat, or, better yet, a non-stuff essential like a week's worth of a diaper delivery service or homemade dinners.

In my own life, I've had the best success in leading by example when it comes to gift-giving. For holidays and birthdays I often give the gift of an experience over a physical object. I might give a gift certificate to a dinner out, or a year's membership to a museum, or a subscription to a paid service like Netflix or Yoga Glo. Whatever the specifics, the key to maintaining a simplified life is to buy into the lifestyle holistically. We can't maintain a clutter-free home if we don't also change our approach to accumulation in the first place.

As with the initial purge, it's easiest to put a halt on trash first when it comes to gatekeeping. Consider the stuff that an average day trip to the grocery store might bring into your home. You buy eggs, milk, and butter. With the exception of the hardworking folks who keep their own chickens and churn their own butter, this means that you've brought into your house not only the foodstuffs, but also the packages they came in and the bag they were put into. Then imagine that you might have had a hankering for a cup of coffee on the way home. Now you've got a coffee cup, too. And then there was the mail to check and among the bills you don't want and the catalogs you never signed up for, there's a free key chain. Outside your door, there are the rain boots you left in the hallway after the last rainstorm. Stuff. Everywhere. And that's just what flurried down after a fifteen-minute trip to the grocery store.

I can't in good conscience suggest that the only solution is for everyone to keep their own flock of chickens. But I can recommend a few good habits for helping to keep the stuff at bay. We'll go over some of these things in greater detail in chapters to come, but here's a partial list:

- Try your best to buy from the bulk section to avoid extra packaging.
- Stop putting your fruits and vegetables into individual plastic bags.
- Bring reusable bags and cups whenever you can.
- Get yourself off junk mail lists through websites like catalogchoice.org.
- Refuse all freebies (swag tables are Enemy #1).
- Set an example: You can't always control what other people give to you, but you can set an example by giving gifts of the edible, usable, experiential variety that you might also hope to receive.

After you've done the hard work of whittling away the excess, it's time to make more careful decisions about what you add back in.

The Hazards of a Storage Unit

A storage unit is a place for someday. And while it might make sense to have a storage unit if you're planning to circumnavigate the globe for a few years and would very much like to return to your creature comforts eventually, the vast majority of things that make their way to a storage unit never make it back out again.

And did you miss them while they were gone?

More often than not, a storage unit puts off the inevitable, which is decluttering. Yes, it's possible and entirely understandable to justify needing extra space. What about the books that you don't have room for now, but that you'll very likely want someday? The clothes your baby outgrew that you want to save for baby-to-be? The holiday decorations that you don't want taking up room in the linen closet all year long? I understand the dilemmas.

But here's the secret: decluttering is a process. Try as you might to decide in one fell swoop those things that must stay, for most of us mortals the process is somewhat more fluid. Deciding what we most love requires revisiting. And a storage unit deprives us of the proximity to make those decisions.

Books
Until very recently, I still had those boxes of books in my parents' attic, patiently awaiting their shining moment in an apartment big enough to display them. Once I did the work of unpacking them, alas, the majority of those books didn't

pass muster. I'd stored—for years—things that I didn't want or need, and they lingered precisely because they were put away where I couldn't see them. Unseen, the books remained. Even the unloved ones. Especially the unloved ones. The treatise on feminist theory that I read over the course of a harried week in graduate school but that I haven't cracked since? Better it serve a current graduate student. The meat-heavy cookbook I've never made a single dish from? The perfect gift for my favorite carnivore.

Holiday Decorations

This might send the folks in charge of the blow-up Santa business into a tailspin of self-doubt, but I propose a new approach to holiday decorating. One that doesn't require a space the size of your bathroom to store. Invest in a few strings of lights that you can tuck into a large shoebox and play up the "boughs of holly" feature of holiday decor by incorporating natural elements that you can compost at the end of the season. Wrap a canvas drop cloth around the base of your Christmas tree. Opt for plain beeswax candles over ones in the shape of dreidel. Drape a live garland on your banister instead of buying a fake one that you'll need to store.

Baby Stuff and Other Things We Save for Someday

I'll admit that some of the baby stuff can most easily masquerade as useful and lovely—who among us can resist tiny sneakers? But here's my best advice: Loan out what you're not currently using, borrow what you can, and return it when you're finished. Be honest with yourself about what was truly useful and what was mere accessory. And when your baby-having days are finished, donate everything. Yes, even the tiny sneakers.

Family Heirlooms: Burdens or Blessings?

Family heirlooms can be delightful things in small quantities and beasts of burden in multiples.

The simple fact is that our stuff outlasts us.

The word *curation* gets thrown around a lot in the lifestyle realm. We hear about curating a gift guide or curating an outfit. In many of these instances the word seems inappropriately applied. But when it comes to our inheritance and our homes, I think that adopting the habits of a curator proves useful, at least in part.

Left to the will of the public, historic house museums would be the final resting places of every sickle, washboard, and butter churn in a fifty-mile radius of that particular museum. As it is, they sometimes are. But the wise museum curator knows that he or she cannot bring every example of a thing into the museum's permanent collection. In Wilmington, North Carolina, I worked as the archivist in precisely this sort of local repository. I spent my days sorting through boxes of donated paperwork, tucking black-and-white photographs into Mylar sleeves, and carefully labeling acid-free folders in pencil so that someone down the line might know their contents. I'm the first to admit that personal artifacts and keepsakes can have important and broad cultural significance. And yet a careful curator must pick and choose the things that a museum acquires based on criteria like age, provenance, ubiquity, and condition. We should do the same thing when it comes to acquiring heirlooms and saving personal ephemera.

Dealing with family heirlooms is complicated in part because of the emotional life wrapped into our things. Again, we should look to the museum curator. The curator understands that an object's value has less to do with precious materials than it does with story. A turned table leg is but a piece of wood until you find that a certain Chippendale had his hand in the mix, and suddenly that wood takes on a different value. Likewise, a tattered top hat is an outmoded bit of haberdashery until one learns that it once sat upon a presidential head. This isn't to suggest that everyone reading this might have rare museum-quality pieces of Americana to contend with. But the principles behind the two examples are good ones to keep in mind. Is there a story behind that heirloom worth telling? You might come into possession of a perfectly average Formica table, purchased at Macy's in the middle of the last century. Its design and materials and condition are not notable. But it was used regularly by your grandmother to make her Sunday roast on. That table, no doubt, has significant value to you personally if not considerable monetary value.

But before you decide that every item in your grandmother's house is one that holds significant meaning for you, consider the next parameter, the one the museum curator *isn't* dealing with: Is it useful? Our homes, after all, are not museums. They are practical spaces where sometimes hard and often joyful work gets done. Is the Formica table one that you could use in your home? Or do you have plans to shunt it to a storage unit or stash it in a basement? Do you already have a table that you don't want to part with? Is the Formica table one that will serve you as the place for family dinners, afternoon homework sessions, and late-night present wrapping? If it is, then keep it. If it's not, and especially if it's something that you plan to "save for later," think twice about keeping it in your home.

This lamp was made out of a crystal candlestick sometime in the last century. It was in my childhood bedroom growing up and in my grandmother's home before that.

This telephone table is an example of a piece of family furniture that was passed down. The original dark-brown finish didn't match the rest of our furniture, but a simple coat of gray paint helped make the piece feel right for our home.

When it comes to family heirlooms, I like to ask myself these questions: Is it useful? Is it lovely? Does it fill a void? If the answer to all three of those questions is *yes*, then I keep the item and put it to good use. If I don't like something, can't imagine using it, or simply don't need it, I store up the memory and story, but part with the physical object. Difficult? Yes. Necessary to keeping my home free of clutter? Yes.

One more note about value: most of us are not material culture experts or antiques appraisers. And as a result, more often than not we assign imaginary value to things that are not terribly valuable. Shows like *Antiques Roadshow* instill the fear—or excitement—that we might all be sitting on a rare and valuable antique, when the opposite is more likely true. If you own something that you think might be of considerable value, by all means get it appraised. But if you're keeping something in your house based on the belief that it *might* be valuable, that's probably not reason enough to keep it.

In my brother-in-law's family, for instance, it was believed that a certain set of 1940s rattan porch furniture was purchased by his great-grandparents while in Australia on a spectacular around-the-world voyage and shipped home to the American Midwest as a souvenir of the adventure. On further investigation, however, it turned out that the set had been purchased at a Sears in Iowa. Suddenly, holding onto the furniture felt less imperative. The story itself became the keepsake.

Donation Guidelines

So now you have bags full of things that you no longer need but that might be perfectly serviceable to someone else. Here are a few resources:

Books
Large charitable organizations like the Salvation Army and Goodwill both accept book donations. Libraries often have "Friends of the Library" book sales that accept donations; check with your local library for more details. There are also a number of terrific nonprofits committed to collecting and redistributing books. Books for Africa (booksforafrica.org) collects reference books and textbooks for primary and secondary school students. Books Through Bars (booksthroughbars.org) collects books to distribute to prisoners at correctional facilities. Books for Soldiers (booksforsoldiers.com) collects books to send to U.S. troops serving overseas. Remember that different organizations have different needs, so always check individual guidelines before dropping off a pile of books.

Clothing
Clothing that's still in good shape can be donated to local thrift stores and national charitable organizations like the Salvation Army and Goodwill. Textile donation drop-offs also sometimes crop up at farmers' markets in larger cities and in suburban parking lots, so keep your eyes peeled for those, too. Consider

also investing in products from manufacturers who have cradle-to-grave recycling policies, like Patagonia, which will repair damaged items and accept returns of no-longer-usable items for responsible recycling.

Electronics

Electronics are filled with materials that shouldn't go into the landfill (lead, cadmium, mercury, and nickel, to name a few). Many cities have electronics recycling programs, so a good place to check for local recycling is through your own municipal website. Other websites like Call2Recycle (call2recycle.org) and Earth911 (earth911.com) have easy-to-use features that allow you to enter the particulars about your electronic device and help you find the best way to get rid of it. As stated above, many manufacturers, like Apple, also accept used and broken items for recycling.

The books that we keep in our house are generally true favorites. Everything else gets borrowed from the library or read and then donated. Our neighborhood happens to have an informal book sharing economy, where people leave books on their stoops for others to scoop up.

What Do I Need to Keep?
A Practical List

The list of paper documents that the average person needs to keep at home feels enormous at first pass, but it is much simpler after closer inspection. In an age when most things have gone digital, there's less need to lug around a paper trail. Here's a quick guide:

Things you can't digitize:
Birth Certificate
Marriage License
Passport
Social Security Card

Things you can digitize:
Bank statements
Bills
Medical records
Pay stubs
Receipts
Tax returns
Transcripts
W-2s

Things you might be holding on to that you don't need to:

Boxes of old or canceled checks

Expired warranties

Instruction manuals for things you no longer own (or for things you already know how to use)

Pay stubs (can be shredded yearly after using to cross-check W-2s)

A small file box is all we need to keep our essential documents in a tidy spot. Everything else gets tossed or digitized.

02:

Simplifying

02:   Simplifying

How do you simplify in a world that's so complicated? Where kitchen gadgets blink and squawk? Where foods come with novel-length ingredient lists? Where our clothing circles the globe before landing in our drawers? How do we go about keeping things simple? Where do we begin? And if we do begin, does it make a difference?

I think it might be helpful to return to the original simplicity seeker, Henry David Thoreau. In reaction to the rapid industrialization he saw around his hometown of Concord, Massachusetts, Thoreau decided to step away for a while. Here are his famous words:

> "I went to the woods because I wished to live deliberately, to front only the essential facts of life, and see if I could not learn what it had to teach, and not, when I came to die, discover that I had not lived. I did not wish to live what was not life, living is so dear; nor did I wish to practice resignation, unless it was quite necessary. I wanted to live deep and suck out all the marrow of life, to live so sturdily and Spartan-like as to put to rout all that was not life, to cut a broad swath and shave close, to drive life into a corner, and reduce it to its lowest terms."[1]

In his quest for simplicity, Thoreau decided to leave his old life behind. He built a cabin in the woods; he prowled around Walden Pond. He scribbled copious notes: detailed

records of plant flowering dates, among other natural phe-
nomena. Mostly, he gnashed his teeth and tried to make sense
of things.

   A century and a half's worth of critics have noted that
he also sometimes left the woods. They have likened what he did
at the edge of the woods in Concord to a young child packing a
bandanna, tying it to a stick, and running away . . . to the end
of the driveway. Yes, Thoreau went to the woods to find the
essentials. But when he was wanting for creature comforts, he
did not hesitate to make a beeline for his friend Ralph Waldo
Emerson's dining table, smack in the center of town.

A single stem of forced
cherry blossoms acts as a
simple bit of decoration
on a wooden crate.

I don't find this inconsistency troubling, nor hypocritical. I find it encouraging. We can, each of us, seek out a simpler mode of doing things. We can do so without abandoning our life as we know it. We can, as Walt Whitman would agree, quite happily contradict ourselves: "I am large, I contain multitudes." We can choose to brew coffee in a French press (no electricity! no doo dads!) and then work all day on computers that allow us to transmit our words across oceans. Just because some elements of our lives are complicated doesn't mean that *every* element of our days needs to be complicated. We get to choose.

Modern (In)Conveniences

Part of living simply, for me, has been recalibrating my definition of convenience.

There are some things that I do on a daily basis, for instance, that might not be defined as convenient. Changing my daughter's cloth diapers, reaching for a cloth rag instead of a paper towel, toting around a stainless-steel water bottle and a cloth grocery bag whenever I leave the house. There are more convenient options. But in each case, the alternative is something that's made to be disposed of. Disposable diapers, paper towels, plastic bags, paper cups—all of these get relegated to a landfill where they're out of sight and out of mind, but they are certainly not without impact.

I am not a Luddite, nor a saint. I have a smartphone that's nearly always slipped into a pocket or bag that I'm carrying around. I have used it to order take-out sushi that comes in disposable containers. I don't always remember my reusable bag. I sometimes eat blueberries in December. I haven't mastered the art of only washing my hair with apple cider vinegar. This is not supposed to be a book in which I share only my fully evolved self. I'm a work in progress.

Here's the truth: Your paper-towel habit won't be the thing that causes environmental doom. We need to do better than not using paper towels. We need to do better than eschewing plastic wrap. We need policies and we need politicians and scientists to work together. We need a paradigm shift. But until that happens, we're not powerless. And I do think that a change in our individual behaviors will finish by making a difference.

Enough about me—take my dad as an example. My dad is creature of habit. He's a wake-up-early, make-a-cup-of-coffee, read-the-*New-York-Times*-before-heading-into-his-home-office kind of guy. He works for a few hours and then he comes back into the kitchen and makes himself peanut butter and toast on a paper plate. Or he used to.

I cut simple cotton rags from T-shirts that have become too stained to wear.

Some New York City Greenmarkets accept all fruit and vegetable food scraps along with other organic matter like coffee grounds, tea bags, eggshells, fresh and dried flowers, and houseplants. In your town, you might find public composting at your own local farmers' market, community garden, or city transfer station.

We didn't use a lot of paper plates in our house growing up, but we always had a stack of them. A just-in-case stack for having friends over or taking on picnics. It was also a stack that my dad reached for most mornings. Happily, a paper plate habit is easily broken: My mom and dad simply stopped buying them.

In fact, when it comes to paper plates, this is especially easy. Chances are that you have a cabinet or shelf full of plates that require washing. Use those instead. Get rid of the alternatives. Or pack the leftovers into a picnic basket for when the occasion actually merits their use. Like my dad, you might grumble about the sudden lack of an option that you can toss into the garbage instead of the dishwasher. But after a day or two of habit-breaking, the Band-Aid will be ripped off.

The same goes for paper towels, except that you might not have the long-lasting equivalent at the ready. In my own house, we keep a basket full of rags. I'd recommend having a supply of at least twenty. After we use our rags, we rinse them off, wring them dry, and once they've mostly air-dried, we stick them into the hamper for a proper washing when we do our weekly load. Once you have the ritual down, it becomes second nature.

We all have a different tolerance for these kind of measures. But I think the point is to stretch beyond your comfort zone a bit. If you're convinced that paper towels are the only thing that works to wipe the avocado smears off your infant's cheeks, experiment with going without for a month. And then think about the garbage you've eliminated from your daily routine.

In fact, many of the inconveniences that I have managed to incorporate into my daily routine have finished by becoming more convenient. *More* simple. And gentler on the planet to boot.

Take composting as an example. James and I started composting when we moved to Brooklyn. It might sound like a strange phenomenon that a move to the city precipitated us finally doing something useful with our food scraps. But a robust collection service run by the New York City Greenmarket made composting so easy that *not* doing it felt like more of a hassle.

Composting food scraps (or saving them for someone else to compost, as we do!) has the double advantage of turning waste into something useful and ensuring less smelly garbage. In the tiny kitchen trash can we've squeezed into our city apartments, even an onion peel quickly makes the whole room stink. Instead of contending with an overripe trash can, we keep a lidded plastic bucket in our freezer. We fill it up with carrot greens and strawberry hulls and coffee grounds. Freezing the scraps means they don't smell as they accumulate over the course of the week. On the weekend, we make a trip to the farmers' market toting our bucket along with us. We empty it, rinse it, and begin the week fresh. It's also meant I can keep our petite trash can under the sink, making more room in our teensy kitchen and reminding us about the waste that we produce. When I find myself emptying the trash too frequently I'm more likely to consider what I'm throwing away.

Take another example. In the summertime, we choose to go without air conditioning. It might seem crazy, as New York City summers are not cool. But not having an air conditioning unit means we don't have to find a place to store it in the off-season. We don't have to block up one of our few windows with the bulky appliance, and we never have a huge spike in electricity costs come July. It's an inconvenience that's ended up not being so inconvenient.

Objects

In my own home, I've made a conscious decision to keep the things in it—appliances to linens—simple themselves, even the hardworking ones. Especially the hardworking ones. The corkscrew, the coffee maker, the can opener. There are electronic versions of each of these things. But I've opted for the simpler choices and found more room, less wrangling, and actual moments of ritual.

Take my morning cup of coffee. There are coffee makers with clocks that can be set to brew the night before. There are others with more knobs and dials and mysterious attachments than the average flying car. But I prefer the simplicity of a French press. Made of glass and metal and bit of mesh, the machine itself is simple. It's a design that's existed for nearly a century without needing improvement or innovation. It doesn't beep or blink at me. It doesn't need an outlet or take up much room on the counter. It's not a thing of exceptional beauty, but it's nice to look at. Making the coffee itself? It offers a moment of calm. I can stand at the kitchen counter groggy-eyed and

Starting the morning off with a cup of coffee in a simple white mug is a ritual I never get tired of.

getting used to a new day as the water heats on the stove. The kettle whistles. I pour hot water over fresh coffee grounds. As the water burbles in, the grounds float up. If I don't rush away, I can stand for a moment and watch them fall down again like a coffee grounds ballet. A few minutes later: a satisfying plunge and a steamy hot cup with a bit of chocolaty froth on top.

Our corkscrew is similarly simplistic. Ours is one that I purchased as a gift to James. It's made from steel and olive wood and was made in France, where I bought it before we had an apartment to put it in. Now, five apartments later, it still works beautifully on the first try every single time.

Far from lacking sentimentality over the things in my house, I actually feel a kind of reverence for them. They've been carefully chosen and considered. When I think about adding

a new thing to my home, I think first of its beauty, second of its utility, and finally of its staying power. Objects that have a timeless appeal are my favorite things: a set of linen napkins, simple white plates, wooden spoons.

To be sure, there are technological advancements that also have a way of simplifying our lives. Our radio is equipped with Bluetooth capabilities that allow it to play digital music files stored on our computer or streamed from our phones. This not only cuts down on the number of wires we have dangling around; it also means that our music collection can be digitized and still enjoyed on stereo speakers. But we've still opted for a machine that's classic in design and elegant in its simplicity.

A metal fan in a classic, attractive design was one of our first splurges as a new couple. We keep this one on the dresser at the foot of our bed year-round. It doubles as an impromptu dryer for wet little socks, and a sound muffler for a sleeping baby.

Wedding Registries

In the decades since my own mother was visiting department stores and carefully selecting china, much has changed in the world of building wedding registries. No longer limited to only fine china and silver, a wedding registry is viewed as an opportunity to fill a home with every conceivable convenience. The shift away from china and silver is often talked about as a turn away from unnecessary convention toward practicality and usefulness. Why ask wedding guests to buy you an expensive formal table setting when those might be closeted away and a simpler, sturdier set is better put to use for your own growing family? Why have a ten-piece sterling silver setting, when all you really use is a stainless steel knife, fork, and spoon? Agreed, on all counts.

And yet, I think something has gotten lost in translation. To replace all of the silver and china, engaged couples are selecting every imaginable kitchen, bed, and bath implement they could ever hope to dream of putting to use. Indeed, the registries are purposefully designed this way. At large box stores, sales associates are trained to encourage registry shoppers to add goods from every department, instead of sticking to only finery. Engaged couples create wish lists that include big-ticket items like a food processor, a blender, an electric mixing bowl, and all manner of much smaller items. In many of these stores, handheld scanners allow shoppers to walk up and down the aisles, scanning goods to add to their registries.

A stack of our simple
white dishes.

The system not only allows, but actively encourages, consumption over consideration, ringing up instead of thinking over. It's no wonder that these lists become jammed with things that go unused or unloved.

Instead of approaching a wedding registry from the perspective of acquiring goods that will—with any luck—last for a lifetime, the approach has become more about making sure to take advantage of an opportunity to get as much as possible. Engaged couples are filling up their lists with affordable items because they're told they need to have a selection of price points. We're stocking our lists with expensive items because we're told we might never have another opportunity.

On principle, the idea of a wedding registry is one that I really appreciate. Having an opportunity to accept from your closest friends and relatives a collection of lovely things you most want and need is a rare and wonderful opportunity. As someone who carefully weighs my decisions about what I bring into my home, I love gifts.

When I was compiling my own wedding registry I used an online registry service at myregistry.com that allowed us to pull choices from a variety of shops and businesses so that I could pick and choose from companies I'd admired for their thoughtful selection of goods instead of being forced into one-stop-shopping at a single store.

My iteration of wedding china is a rustic set of plain white dishes, handmade in the United States. It isn't precious per se, but it is precious to me. Despite the fact that we were living in incredibly close quarters, James and I registered for ten place settings. Miraculously, when unpacked from their boxes, these too managed to fit into our tiny apartment. We boxed up our old dishes and sent them off to my younger sisters to use in their own first apartments.

In addition to those plates, we made a few additional requests for napkins, cutlery, an enameled cast-iron Dutch oven, and an improved heavy-bottomed saucepan, as well as a few classic kitchen utensils. These were all things that I knew we would use and, more importantly, things that we wouldn't grow tired of. By and large, we added things whose original design has endured. A metal ice cream scoop. A simple pizza cutter. A set of plain dish towels—cream with a thick blue stripe. Tested by time, not trends.

To be sure, my own wedding registry wasn't perfect. We included very pretty but mildly impractical cutlery that takes up a lot of bulk and needs to be hand-washed. We chose a color for our Dutch oven that I might someday want to change. But mostly, we used the registry as a way to add special pieces that we knew we'd use for a lifetime. We wanted to put our gifts to work.

And when we already owned something that worked perfectly well, we decided not to register for the new version. Instead of replacing the stained yellow stand-mixer that belonged to James's mom before us, we kept the vintage version. You can't really put family stories on a wedding registry, but in a way, we did.

More than anything else, I think that one of the sweetest gestures each of us can make when embarking on a new marriage is to fill a registry with things made to survive evolutions of style and trends and the chaos of ensuing decades. Indeed, it's the same hope that we have for our marriages themselves.

Marriage in the works or not, I've included my list of basic items that I've found to be helpful in a tiny home or otherwise on the following pages.

Nearly forty years later, this stand-mixer is still going strong.

Kitchen Essentials

White dishes: The little black dress of china, a white plate can be dressed up or dressed down but will never go out of style. As the classic LBD advice goes: Look for a shape that appeals to you, in a sturdy material, with few adornments. We chose handmade dishes with a creamy white glaze.

Plain café-style glasses: Classic French Duralex glasses are heavy-duty, functional, and affordable. We use these for everything from water and juice to wine and lattes. The smallest size is just right for a tiny toddler grip.

Cutlery: Go with stainless steel or silver, both of which can be put in the dishwasher and should last for decades—if not centuries. We have a beautiful set of wooden-handled stainless-steel cutlery that will last longer if hand-washed. Done again, I might opt for a set of vintage silverware to use every day that doesn't need to be specially handled. But then again, practicality can't *always* win.

Cast-iron pans: Well-seasoned cast-iron pans are virtually nonstick, a source of iron, and workhorses in the oven or on the stovetop. Vintage cast iron can be pricey but has the advantage of being very well-seasoned and smooth-bottomed. Brand-new Lodge pans are incredibly affordable. Both will quite literally last forever.

Stainless-steel saucepans: We have a 4-quart and a 6-quart pan that we use near-daily for everything from boiling water for pasta to simmering sauces and reheating leftovers.

Cast-iron Dutch oven: In the land of one-pot cooking, nothing compares to a classic, enameled Dutch oven. And they can be just as good secondhand as brand-new. We use ours for simmering stews and chilis and baking bread. In a pinch, it can multitask as an ice bucket or a baby bathtub.

Simple Duralex tumblers are equally good for water and wine, and are practically indestructible.

Wooden cutting board: A thin wooden cutting board kept well-oiled and clean is the only one you need.

A set of knives: In a truly minimalist kitchen, you can probably get away with just one or two good chef's knives. We use a 5-inch Santoku knife that we love, but I recommend going to a neighborhood kitchen shop and trying out a few to determine which one feels best in your hand. To save counter space and protect our knives from damage, we use a magnetic knife rack attached to the wall.

Microplane: I'm still waiting for a beautiful wooden-handled version to make it to market, but a Microplane is a useful tool in any kitchen. Good for lemon zesting and cheese grating without taking up much room.

Stainless-steel sheet pans: Our tiny apartment oven is too small to fit a regular-size cookie tray, so we use jelly roll pans as baking sheets. Whatever the size, I've had the best luck with uncoated stainless-steel sheet pans. You can use them for everything from roasting vegetables to baking cookies. With only a bit of care, they won't warp, and they take scratches and nicks and everyday wear with gusto.

Measuring cups and spoons: Some things do call for a little precision. A one-cup liquid measure and a set of dry measures is all we use, plus a set of measuring spoons. All of them are stainless steel, utilitarian, and sturdy. (If space is an issue, a standard 8-ounce mason jar can stand in for a one-cup liquid measure.)

Mixing bowls: Whether tempered glass, stainless steel, or sturdy stoneware, a solid set of mixing bowls is useful for all manner of recipes, and an attractive set can do double-duty as serving bowls.

Toxins

The word *natural* gets thrown around a lot, but what does it mean? Nothing—and everything. Unlike official certifications, the "natural" label is more or less marketing jargon. It can be used to describe all manner of things that are decidedly *not* natural. And not everything that comes from the earth is inherently good for us. I don't recommend licking lead or bathing in sulphur, though both appear on the periodic table.

I'm the first to admit that it can actually feel simpler to bury your head in the sand than to parse what exactly is safe. There's an awful lot of fear-mongering. There's an awful lot of conflicting data. And there's an awful lot of greenwashing—that fine art of making something sound natural when it is not. But in the midst of all of this noise, some things are actually knowable. And in this case, ignorance turns out to be not-so-blissful. Here again, some of the answer lies in simply going without.

As an example, plastics are everywhere we look. They line our shopping shelves, we put them dutifully into our recycling bins and some of them get reused in a process that requires nearly as many resources as their original production did.

I moved into my first adult apartment at a fortuitous time when conversation about plastics and BPA and the hazards of both were just starting to get attention. James and I traded our plastic water bottles for stainless-steel ones. We bought glass containers to store our foods. We do our best to avoid single-use plastic as much as possible, but we also avoid plastic generally, opting for wooden or stainless-steel alternatives for a whole range of tools, utensils, and kitchen implements.

Here's why: There are bad plastics and worse plastics and plastics that can't get recycled. BPA—bisphenol A—got quite a bit of attention several years ago, when it was determined to be in everyone's favorite plastic water bottle. A known endocrine disruptor that mimics the hormone estrogen, BPA also lines aluminum cans and has been found in hard plastics ranging from baby bottles to bottle caps. The BPA leaches out of the plastic and into our food and, ultimately, into our bodies. Plastics with a number 3 or 7 imprinted on the bottom are most likely to include BPA and, as a rule, should be avoided.

But because nothing is truly simple, the attention paid to creating BPA-free plastics has led to the production of alternative plastics that are indeed BPA-free but that include *other* endocrine disruptors that are just as bad. Ready to bury your head in the sand yet? Me too.

Instead, let's just go cold turkey. You might have trouble eliminating every single bit of plastic from your life, but it's easy to drastically reduce your reliance on it, quickly:

Ways to Avoid Plastic:

- Buy in bulk using cloth produce bags to cart home dried goods
- Use a reusable mug made from stainless steel or ceramic
- Choose wooden and stainless-steel utensils
- Refuse plastic water bottles; fill up a stainless-steel bottle instead
- Bring your own bag or basket to the grocery store and farmers' market
- Opt for items sold in cardboard packaging over plastic
- Shop locally to avoid plastic packaging in shipping materials

I'll talk a bit more about materials in the chapter on decorating (page 90), but I think the standard to strive for is simple materials: wood and steel and fibers like wool and linen and cotton.

Allies

In the quest for simplicity a person needs allies. In choosing to live with less, it's important to have people on your team. People who understand the motivation to weed out the excess, but also people who can give a nudge or offer a bit of advice or push you in the right direction. We're faced with so many

We received a beautiful set of linen napkins for our wedding. Linen napkins sometimes get a bad rap as difficult to care for, but I've found that they've gotten much softer with use, and unless there's a special occasion, I don't bother with ironing.

So many standard kitchen utensils are produced in plastic these days, but keeping wooden handles well-fed with a combination of beeswax and coconut oil keeps them in terrific shape and much more beautiful than their plastic counterparts.

choices, it's important to find allies who can help do some of the work for us.

For me, those allies have taken different shapes. Sometimes it's been a sister challenging me to break an old habit or form a new one. Other times it's been a documentary film or a magazine article that's made me feel buoyed in an endeavor to go against the grain. It's been book authors, certainly. But it's also been merchants: farmers selling their goods at the market and small business owners stocking thoughtful products.

When James and I were first living in North Carolina, after months of living in town, we found an out-of-the-way food co-op that became a little oasis for us as we started to make decisions about the kinds of foods and products we wanted to bring into our home.

Before I found the co-op, I admit that I'd developed something that I jokingly call shopping paralysis. I'd walk into a conventional grocery store and fill my cart, but then I'd look down at what I'd accumulated and begin to tick off what I'd learned. The tomatoes are in a can that might have BPA in it. The plastic wrap around those mushrooms won't biodegrade. The celery certainly wasn't grown without copious amounts of pesticide. I'd circle back around the store, returning things to their shelves like a proper weirdo. At the co-op, I felt more secure in my decisions in part because someone else had helped me make them.

James and I have found similar allies in the local natural food and co-op grocery stores in each city we've lived in. These shops have helped us by making purchasing and stocking decisions that bar from entry a whole slew of things that we never have to sort through. They've been the places where we could buy items in bulk—from herbs to teas to whole grains and dried nuts. They've had refill stations for soaps and olive oils and maple syrup. They've accepted glass bottle returns for milk and beer. When we don't have the time or energy to take the from-scratch route, they're places where it's easy to seek out products that have been responsibly made by someone else.

Less close to home, over the past few years I've found allies in online businesses stocking products with an eye toward longevity, usefulness, and beauty. To be sure, some of this still comes down to consumption. I don't really *need* a beautiful stoneware planter, but knowing that the shop that stocks it exists when it *is* time to make the purchase can be a helpful thing to know. And maybe best of all, beyond the shops stocking other people's wares, the Internet has provided a platform for all sorts of people to sell their own goods directly. When I buy from the person who has made something themselves, the act of consuming the product feels meaningful beyond my own immediate satisfaction. Knowing that I'm supporting the work of someone else directly is actually something to feel proud of.

When approaching the stuff of your home and making decisions about what to add, seek out your allies. Find people who are embarking on a similar path and throw your energy their way.

Beautiful Messes

Not everything can always be tucked away, and messes are certainly in the eye of the beholder. A friend of mine used to joke that I'd say that my room was a mess if there was an errant sock on the floor. Point taken. But finicky personal habits aside, there's one rule of thumb that I've found to be helpful when I approach new purchases. If left strewn about, would this thing be considered an object of beauty or an eyesore?

I just felt your eyes roll, but bear with me. You're in control of your space. It's an idea that's so radical I think most of us just choose to ignore it. But imagine a home where you actually enjoyed looking at everything in it. From throw blankets, to toys, to books, to sponges, to cereal boxes, to shopping bags, to teethers, to sun hats, to picnic coolers. I admit to thinking about the aesthetic beauty of a thing before thinking about almost anything else. Trivial? Time-wasting? Not when you

My advice is this: Surround yourself with things of beauty, so that even in its messiest moments, your life still feels beautiful.

consider the broader implication, which is thoughtfulness. The point is to make considered purchases instead of mindless purchases. Some purchases are made from necessity, yes. But I still think that there needs to be more choices that are also born from *enjoyment*. More often than not, when I can't afford the most beautiful version of a thing, I simply go without.

A Note About Babies

There is a nearly limitless list of things that people will tell you that you need when you have a baby. A lot of this sharing comes from a good place. Having a baby is hard work. Living with that baby, caring for the baby, feeding the baby, finding a moment of peace in your own day with a baby? All of that is even harder. It's no surprise that we search for answers. That we try to find a way to make it easier. And when, after a sleepless night, we discover that a pacifier or a sound machine or a certain sleeper blanket made all the difference, we want to shout it

I painted my own childhood changing table white and added new handles before Faye was born.

We added a simple crib to our room when Faye reached about four months and outgrew her Moses basket.

from the rooftops. And certainly, we should share our discoveries. But it's just as important to take them with a grain of salt.

Nothing, not a single thing, makes caring for a baby easy. And what gets made easier by the introduction of some thing or another will depend entirely on the particulars of your baby, your family, and your space.

When we moved into a larger apartment in anticipation of the birth of our daughter, we knew that we could make living in an apartment with just one bedroom possible because we were already committed to living simply. I knew that we wouldn't be investing in playpens or rocking chairs or most of the kinds of baby products that typically get touted as essential. We bought very little in advance. Before Faye was born, we got a small Moses basket for her to sleep in. We welcomed a dresser that had been bought by my parents in the eighties and used in my own childhood home through four kids, and then was used by my nephew. I painted it white and made new leather drawer pulls. It serves the purpose of changing table and repository for diapers and tiny clothes, and it's also a reminder that for every midnight diaper change that we muscle through, there have been countless others in this very same space. We eventually bought a simple crib and a second-hand organic mattress. We decided to use a wooden high chair that had belonged to James and had been stored in the attic of his childhood home by his hopeful parents. Other things, we decided to go without.

**Simplifying
Baby Gear**

Unable to choose a baby swing or bouncer that met our dual criteria of being pleasant to look at and affordable, we forwent one altogether. For the few short months—or was it mere weeks?—when we might have used one, we made do with wearing our daughter in a carrier or sling inside the house. When we needed to set her down, we put her to sleep in a lambskin-lined Moses basket. I propped Faye on a throw pillow instead of buying a pillow specially designed to help with breastfeeding. I made my own version of a play gym—hanging

A set of hand-painted blocks in front of Faye's dresser.

wooden rings from a tripod made from wooden dowels. I set up a cozy spot for Faye to practice "tummy time" on a soft blanket, but I didn't purchase a mat specifically designed for the purpose. On the advice of our babysitter, I fed her frozen blueberries when she was teething and popped a rubber spatula in the freezer for her to suck on.

If you feel overwhelmed by the choices in baby gear, you *can* simply opt out. At the very least, you can stall the onslaught by deciding to wait and see what you might end up needing rather than making many purchases in advance. (If you have a kindly neighbor who would like to unload all of their unused baby gear on you, you can politely decline.)

In my experience, the preferences and habits of our own tiny baby changed so rapidly in those early months that by the time I thought a swing or a bouncy chair might be helpful, she was already on to something else—sleeping in a different pattern, or exploring our apartment in a new way, or suddenly interested in a spoon or book or colander that we already owned and that could occupy her better than anything we'd be able to buy new. For my part, I found having less made things easier. I never felt overwhelmed by baby gear because I never really had much.

We decided against having a baby shower in part because I wanted to keep our baby supplies to a minimum. But at my mom's urging I put together a pared-down online registry and pulled together a few things I had my eye on—mostly adorable baby clothes and bigger-ticket items like a carrier and a stroller, which friends and family pooled resources to buy.

Minimalist Baby Toys

The Los Angeles study I referenced earlier indicates that "U.S. buyers are responsible for annually purchasing a mind-boggling 40 percent of the world's toys."[2] In hopes of making even a tiny dent in that number and simultaneously keeping our sanity in a small apartment, we've kept Faye's toys to a minimum. Borrowing from Montessori and Waldorf traditions, which value order and creative play, we've compiled for Faye a small

collection of simple wooden toys, a cloth doll, a classic teddy bear, a couple of musical instruments and a collection of board books to engage her during the day.

I've let friends and family know (gently) that I'm hoping not to introduce many toys into our home, and gifts we've received have been lovely and thoughtful, and yes, minimal. Because we live in a small space, it's clear to all that there are only so many stuffed animals a tiny apartment can hold—and that a single child can enjoy. But no matter what kind of space you live in, in moments when you start to be overwhelmed, you can do as we have done: donate duplicate items or rotate a selection of toys to a spare closet, to bring them out later. Some of this has felt like common sense. But I've also loved psychologist Kim John Payne's wise words on the subject:

> We are the adults in our children's lives. We are the grown-ups. And as the parents who love them, we can help our children by limiting their choices. We can expand and protect their childhoods by not overloading them with the pseudochoices and the false power of so much *stuff*. And as companies spend billions trying to influence our children, we can say no. We can say no to entitlement and overwhelm, by saying yes to simplifying.[3]

Faye's dedicated toys and books are relegated to a small shelf and a crate under our couch. But we've also rearranged our apartment in such a way that she has ample room to safely investigate all manner of playthings and curiosities we'd never imagined as toys—until she deemed them so. In other words: While we haven't let baby stuff overrun our apartment, other things have *become* baby stuff. Our salad spinner? It's delivered whole minutes of absorbed fun. Wooden spoons and saucepans? Instant drums. With an attentive adult nearby, our kitchen chairs have served as makeshift baby walkers.

Of course, at the time of writing, our baby is less than a year old. Her needs are similarly small. As she continues to grow, no doubt, so will these things. But I think that that growth can be slow. Slower, perhaps, even than the growth of the child. Which, as any new parent will tell you, is rapid. I'm hopeful that as she gets older there will be an emphasis on games of the imagination, on exploring outside, on making art and getting dirty. But right this minute, we're getting all sorts of mileage out of a tower of wooden blocks and a set of stainless-steel measuring cups snagged from a kitchen cabinet.

Faye's toys kept wrangled in a box.

Newborn Essentials

Because most lists of newborn essentials are a mile long, here's one that's slightly shorter:

Cotton onesies: There are all kinds of adorable things for suiting up the smallest set among us, but by far my favorite is classic white cotton onesies. They're simple, eminently washable, they never go out of style, and they match everything.

Cloth diapers: Whether or not you cloth diaper your child, having a few cotton prefold diapers on hand for cleaning up spills, wiping up spit-up, or slipping underneath a new baby bottom during an impromptu diaper change is a wise thing to add to a new baby registry.

Cotton swaddles: Newfangled swaddles have nothing on classic square muslin swaddling cloths. We borrowed a set from my sister and used them as sunshields on sunny stroller rides, blankets in the park, nursing covers, and rolled-up, as extra support for a first-time breast-feeding mom, in addition to swaddling for sleep.

Lambskin: We call our short-haired wool sheepskin a sheepie and use it constantly. It's easy to clean—you can literally just toss a lambskin in the washing machine with cold water and mild detergent and air-dry it, and it emerges soft and fluffy.

What's more, it's cozy, naturally anti-bacterial, and water- (and other-wet-things) resistant.

Moses basket: We lined our basket with our lambskin and let our daughter doze in it during the day and sleep in it for the first four months or so. Later, we flipped it upside down and Faye practiced standing and walking around its perimeter when she was taking her first steps. Today, we keep it underneath a bench with a baby doll and stuffed bear inside.

Other things: Of course babies need basic daily supplies like diapers and wipes of some kind or another for cleaning up dirty bums. Breastfed or formula-fed babies alike will probably need bottles and nipples. A nursing mother will likely need a breast pump. A diaper bag is helpful eventually, though it doesn't have to be elaborate. A stroller might make long walks easier. In our family, a carrier proved essential. But much of that you can decide on after the baby arrives. Find your rhythm first; then, find the things that match it.

03:

Organizing

03:   Organizing

So you've cleared the clutter. But chances are, there's still some work to be done.

You have fewer shoes, but they're still tossed in the bottom of the closet. You've gotten rid of the moth-eaten sweaters, but the ones you've saved are still thrown willy-nilly on a shelf. The two cookie sheets you decided you can't live without are threatening to avalanche if you open the cabinet door. How do you get it all organized, even when there's less of it?

As a child, I loved looking at catalogs. I would pore over them. Sometimes, when I was alone with my mom—a rarity for a child with three sisters—we would go through the pages of the latest arrival together, cuddled up on the couch, and pick out one thing on each page that we liked the best. I loved the particular neatness of these glossy tableaus. The straight lines and order in each of the rooms. There were never piles of junk mail, or an unruly mound of recyclables waiting to go out to the curb, or heaps of unfolded laundry. The home I grew up in was more or less tidy, but there was something in the sparsity of the catalog images that appealed to me.

You might say that the difference between real life and fantasy lies in the messes. You might argue that in those perfectly styled catalogs we're being sold an idea of perfection that's neither attainable nor even desirable. It's hard to have delicious chocolate-chip cookies without making a mess first. Wine glasses left unwashed in the sink because you stayed up too late chatting with friends are probably a good thing. As my dad would remind me: In the final analysis, no one's going to care whether the laundry got folded.

One can clearly go too far: It's surely more important to write the next great American novel than to reorganize your sock drawer. (Though I find reorganizing the sock drawer sets me up for a good, productive stint of work.) But in paying at least a bit of attention to the way we organize the space we call home, we ultimately save time and energy for the people living in it, and more room—metaphysically or not—for the things that really matter. Maybe even more important, in creating an organized space, we inherently create a more thoughtful space; a space that doesn't allow room for unnecessary consumption.

I have a modest collection of glass bottles. I keep them lined up on one closet shelf. Some of the bottles have been found buried whole in parents' backyards (the ultimate example of one person's trash being another's treasure). Others have been gifts from James—vintage labware that he's been able to snag as old glass gets cycled out of the university laboratories he's worked in. Even though the shelf is hidden behind a closed closet door, I've limited my collection to what I can fit neatly on that closet shelf and still look intentional, not crowded. On my neatly arranged shelf, a new bottle addition wouldn't go unnoticed. In the same way that I don't add more dresses to my closet than I have hangers for, or add a second shampoo bottle when there's only room for one to fit neatly on the edge of the tub—when I prioritize orderliness, I keep unruly additions at bay.

And I'll go further. I think opening a closet door and finding a neat row of glass bottles instead of an over-stuffed mess actually *feels* better. I think how we structure our surroundings plays a role in how we perceive our lives, and how we experience the ebb and flow of stress in our days. Remember that UCLA study? More stuff meant more anxiety and less happiness. Disorganization in a home can be an actual burden. And controlling the chaos of everyday life means not spending our days searching in the far reaches of the attic for the missing extension cord or digging through a graveyard of mismatched Tupperware lids, searching for the perfect fit. Once created, order gives us the opportunity to seek and create peace where we live.

There's Always Storage

Let's start with the assumption that there's always at least a tiny bit of storage. It might not come in the form of a beautifully appointed walk-in closet, or a series of built-in bookshelves. You might have only one dresser, or a tiny bookshelf. But I'll argue that storage—a space available for storing something— is a frame of mind more than anything else.

Here's what I mean: In every new living situation, there's a temptation to rush to the local box store specializing in storage solutions and buy something. It can feel as if all of your troubles will be solved if you just make the perfect purchase. Remember those catalogs? We're conditioned—some of us from a very young age—to think that buying something new will solve a problem. Sometimes buying a new something-or-other *does* make a difference. Sometimes the difference between a closet overrun with shoes and one with shoes that are neatly organized is indeed a shoe rack.

But many storage solutions are limiting. The more drawers and lids and closed-up spaces that we have to stash our things, the more things we accumulate there, out of view. They're temporarily helpful, but in the long-term they're recipes for overstuffed disaster. In our house, we recently divested ourselves of a "cord keeper"—a large bulky box that was meant to orga- nize all of our electrical cords—because we realized that it only actually held three cords, all of which belonged to electronics we no longer owned. Oops. Therein lies the rub.

I find that drawer organizers, silverware trays, shower caddies, and shelf dividers often create a storage problem where there wasn't one before. Take flatware, for example. When we lived in our first North Carolina apartment, we had drawer

space aplenty, and it made sense to tidy up our forks and spoons in one of those standard silverware trays one buys at a hardware store. Then we moved to an apartment with nary a kitchen drawer. The storage "solution" was now a bulky eyesore. It took up space, instead of making good use of it. And so we sorted our flatware into two clean glass jars and stored them at easy arm's reach in an overhead cabinet. They're now faster to put away, just as conveniently located, and make good use of cute jars that were otherwise destined for the recycling bin. We should have never purchased the tray to begin with. When you decide that you don't need to rely on store-bought contraptions, the amount of storage space available to you actually expands, and the pleasure you get from your things increases. More often than not, a little creativity and attention to detail

With limited square footage, we've had luck in using the space below our cot for extra storage. Tall legs allow for ample room, and a simple wooden crate still looks tidy tucked underneath.

can get you the same sense of satisfaction and organization. It's worth pausing before barreling out the door in search of a cure-all.

My spice cabinet also comes to mind. I'd love to have an expertly organized spice cabinet. It would have rows of spices all neatly labeled and equally visible in matching jars. In my dream spice cabinet, I could scan the cabinet and quickly pluck out the cumin. No, in my dream spice cabinet I wouldn't even need to scan. I'd know where the cumin was, fifth from the right, next to the cinnamon.

But living in rental apartments has prevented me from investing in a special rack or built-in stand. I could buy a thirty-five dollar rack from a store full of similar products designed to trick-out kitchen cabinets. But once I move again, the likelihood that that rack would remain useful is slim to none. I'd have to leave it behind, and I'd have to find something new in whatever next place I landed. It's a cycle without an end in sight.

So instead of looking for a storage "solution," I've opted for reducing my storage needs altogether. Instead of stocking dozens of pre-ground spices and dried herbs, I rely heavily on fresh-cut herbs and fresh-ground spices, bought only when I need them. For those few nonperishable spices I like to always have on hand, I keep them in a set of 4-ounce mason jars, easily stackable and scannable.

I'll pause to say that in a house that you own, built-in storage units can undoubtedly be helpful. A closet outfitted with custom pull-out drawers, sized perfectly to fit a folded sweater, has undeniable appeal. Kitchen cabinets sized to fit your cookie sheets? Dreams do come true! If I knew that I would be living in one particular home for a considerable length of time, I would likely invest in or make my own more permanent storage solutions.

Everything in Its Place

Whenever readers of my blog see photographs of my home, I get the inevitable question: "Where's all the stuff?" One particularly incredulous reader once asked why they saw a surfboard in my apartment, but no wetsuit. The answer doesn't lie in smoke and mirrors but in closets and on shelves. Making use of what storage you do have is a crucial step toward not being overwhelmed in a small apartment, but for me it's been necessary for cultivating a sense of calm in any size space.

How to begin?

In my home I have a commitment to keeping the surfaces clear. On my desk, I keep my computer and keyboard. On my dresser I keep a small dish of jewelry and a tiny leather case of glass vials—a special gift from a friend. My nightstand has a small lamp for illuminating bedtime stories. If I happen to have any, a small bit of greenery or a tiny spray of flowers in a glass bottle from the shelf that I keep full of them might be added, but mostly these spaces are kept free of stuff. For me, the daily messes are more manageable if they happen in a place that's not already cluttered.

In our small home, finding a place to store our belongings has sometimes meant stashing things in places that might not make sense to an unversed observer. We keep our toilet paper in our linen closet, which happens to be as far away from our bathroom as you can get. But since our bathroom isn't big enough for a cabinet of its own, it's a solution that works for us. We keep our scissors and matches and twine in the same closet, corralled together in a basket. Be ruthless in your commitment to clear surfaces—when the goal is finding a place to keep everything tucked away (and not buying more stuff to do it) your solutions will surprise and delight you with their idiosyncratic creativity and sense. No one else has to "get it."

Living in close quarters has taught me that multifunctionality isn't reserved for the products that make the claim. Multifunctionality is in the eye of the beholder. Our closet?

It serves the triple function of clothes, utility, and coat closet. Oh, and also baby-changing station, diaper storage spot, and place to hang the coats and bags of visiting grandmas and grandpas.

The key is to be intentional. My vacuum sits at the base of my clothes closet, because there's not another alternative, but it gets returned to the same place after each use. Our dustpan and broom hang from a wall behind my clothes, and they get returned—clean—there after each use, too. In these ways, even though the particular storage spot is unconventional, the actual act of putting items away makes sense and becomes second nature.

Keeping the Little Things Tidy

In any size space, it's ironically the littlest things that cause the biggest headaches. See: those pesky spices! But it's also the loose baby bottle nipples, tiny spoons, the bits and pieces of the mason jar lids, the attachments to a stand mixer, the bottle stoppers. I've found three things to be useful: baskets, bags, and jars. All look nice; all wrangle odds and ends effectively. All smack more of decor than utility, though they're truthfully both. They're proof that you don't need special gadgets or gizmos to stay organized; you need just the habit of putting everything back in its proper place and a few basic supplies for keeping that place tidy.

Hang It Up

A hammer and nails and an occasional hook or two are some of an organized life's most important tools. I can't begin to count the number of times that I have struggled with organization in a particular corner of the apartment, only to remember that the simple addition of a nail or screw would make all the difference. In baby proofing, cord wrangling, and tool keeping, we've used simply hammer, nails, and hooks to hang things in places that are accessible to the right people.

This leather-handled Estwing hammer is an affordable and hardworking hammer that would be pretty enough to keep displayed.

Needing to keep a dust-pan in an unconventional spot, like your clothes closet, doesn't mean that it needs to look out of place. A simple screw in the drywall and a bit of twine through the end of the dustpan helps it look right at home, even when it's nestled among dresses and overcoats.

Useful for canning, the two-piece mason jar lid can be a pain when it comes to using the jars for dry storage. I bought a set of solid metal lids to replace the two-piece canning lids, and I wrangle extras in a small muslin pouch.

We have three small toolboxes in our apartment. My favorite is this one, given to my dad on his tenth birthday.

We've hung our dustpan and hand broom on a bit of twine and a screw in the back wall of the closet. The solution to towels in the bathroom? Two hooks on the back of the door. Curtain rods when you don't want to invest in expensive hardware? Screws and annealed wire. Hiding a surge protector? Two screws on the underside of a table. It goes without saying that sometimes even a temporary fix can have a huge impact.

Organizing often comes down to taking the time to tackle a project, more than having the money to invest in a solution. A good hammer and a few nails have done me more good than most organizing solutions on the market.

Developing Habits

The most organized space is only as organized as the human in charge of keeping it that way. Recall the habit of decluttering? Same goes for organizing.

Consider my desk. It's a table. It doesn't have drawers. I keep my computer, my mouse, and a keyboard on top. While I'm working I might also have a paper calendar (my own Achilles heel in the battle against sentimental stuff). If I need a pen to jot something down, I might retrieve it from the small jar I keep full of pens in my linen closet. I don't keep the jar on my desk, because it makes the space feel crowded. When I'm finished working, I return the pen to its jar. I close my calendar and slip it back into my work bag. I bring my mug to the kitchen sink for washing. Any books that I've been reading for reference get returned to the crate or shelf where they live. My desk is cleared once again. Habits. For me, the reward of a clean desk far outweighs the moment it takes to put everything back in its place. I repeat the same habit with my kitchen counters and dresser tops and dining table.

Our collection of
wooden crates comes
from flea markets in
the different cities
where we've lived.

Using Wooden Crates

After college, I noticed a phenomenon in the first adult apartments of many of my friends. Instead of investing in furniture, we were all, as a generation, using the plastic bins and storage units we'd collected for college moves. Rubbermaid in the service of dresser drawers. Milk crates as nightstands. In the case of one friend, a plastic bin served as a coffee table. And that "coffee table" served as a dining table.

On one hand, I applaud the habit. That plastic is going to stay with us forever, so you might as well keep using it. But in the case that you want your home to have an air of style, however simple, you might consider a different approach to temporary furniture.

In my own home, I rely largely on a collection of recycled wooden crates to serve similar purposes. A wooden crate used as a nightstand might not be everyone's cup of tea. When weighed against a piece of finely crafted furniture, it might appear positively paltry. But for reasons both environmental and aesthetic, I think that they're an improvement over plastic bins. Most important for my own home, they're near endlessly useful. In our house, we've even swapped out small or spindly end tables and side tables for sturdier but compact crates. We've found that a vintage solid-sided crate turned on its end is just the right height for keeping next to a bed or couch and is perfect for tucking away a stack of books that might otherwise be taking up real estate on the tabletop. We've used open-slat crates to wrangle boots by the door and old wine crates to slide underneath our couch. They can be stashed in a closet and turned into makeshift hat storage. And if you move to a new apartment and are left closetless, they're not so bad to look at. They're not fine furniture, but they do a fine job of standing in its place.

Open Storage

We change how we use this bookshelf—a vintage wool slipper crate—depending on our needs. Currently, it stores cookbooks on its lowest shelf, a few well-loved toys for our daughter on the middle shelf, and a few accessories of daily life up top.

Here's a case for open storage. Or maybe one against it. I admit that too much open storage sometimes looks messy to me. In catalogs and on Instagram, beautifully styled kitchens with rustic shelves are often lined with just a smattering of kitchen detritus: a topsy-turvy vintage plate beside a solitary jar of dried beans. A single cocktail stirrer laid aside a coupé glass. But some things are better left to the magazines. In real life, you're likely to have more than one glass and a veritable storeroom of grocery stuffs. And relying solely on open storage means you're likely to see *all* of it, not just the choicest few items. To strike a balance between the romance of open shelving and the practicalities of a working kitchen, I find that a combination of simple open storage and buttoned-up belongings creates the most harmony in a home.

Open storage can be useful because by default it makes you consider what you accumulate in your home. If the only option for storing mugs is an open shelf, you might be less tempted to dip into the swag table at that conference or double-up on the bar mitzvah favors.

In any case, keep your storage intentional. Intentional storage might indeed result in intentional purchases and keep the very need for storage in check.

04:

Decorating

04:   Decorating

Mine is a decorating philosophy about living with what you love, filling your home with objects that have personal significance, and barring from entry anything superfluous. This chapter tackles decorating with an eye toward

sustainability and economy. It's not about interior design per se. It won't include decorating rules or color swatches or ratios or anything else that I imagine a real designer might offer. It's about creating a home that's simple and sustainable, slowly.

Light and Bright

I spent an inordinate amount of time in colonial house museums as a child. Growing up in southern New England, every town near the one I grew up in boasted one such place. When I was ten, my mom researched and wrote her first in a series of travel guides to New England, and as a result my sisters and I had the advantage of being toted around with her as she toured many of these homes. Something about the Puritan aesthetic stuck with me—all of those historic homes with neatly swept floors and chairs pushed to the edges of the room.

Surely, some of this stems from the very fact that these were museums. And yes, I see the problem here. Museums are for looking at, not for living in. Surely it bears repeating: Life is messy, and real life in colonial America was no doubt quite messy. Filthy, even. But I still like to borrow from this simple aesthetic when I design the places where I live. I like to have the bare necessities, little that's extraneous, and plenty of room for pushing the furniture aside and having a big old dance party, or building a pillow fort, or carving pumpkins in the middle of the apartment floor.

For me, the key to creating a calm, spare, and livable space has always been to err on the side of keeping a space light and bright. Two simple rules, but they go a long way.

First, to keep my apartments visually bright, I've usually left the untinted white that landlords favor. (This saves money, too.) I like the idea of starting with a neutral palette and adding bits of color sparingly. I have a few favorite prints framed. I have

The mirror on our antique
dresser has desilvered
a bit, but it still reflects
light from our windows
and bounces it back into
the room.

We replaced an ugly
ceiling light with a simple
white fixture from
Schoolhouse Electric that
completely transformed
the room.

others that are merely taped to the wall. But in general, I like
to leave plenty of white space.

For the "light" part, I try not to bring anything into a
space that doesn't give off light, catch the light, extend the
light, or direct attention to light. So in places we've lived,
depressing overhead lighting either gets replaced or never
turned on. Windows, if we cover them at all, get hung with
partially sheer curtains that let in morning sun and catch the
glow of the afternoon magic hour. A big mirror hung opposite
those windows helps reflect more light around the room.
A light-colored bedspread in a shadowy bedroom works
against the gloom. In our most recent move, we repainted our
bedroom furniture a deep navy blue. Not bright, but just right
for making a stark contrast with surrounding light we made
sure was there.

I concede entirely that on first glance, my home is not
a riot of color. But on closer inspection, I think my focus on
keeping things light and bright means you can spot the color
better when it does appear. Like the pop of seasonal color
that comes with a bit of foraged greenery. Or the tiny flowers
from the neighborhood bodega that do the trick of freshening
up the place without my needing to invest in anything that
I'll need to store later, or feel guilty about no longer loving a
few years down the line. The dim recess of the kitchen, made
brighter with a bowl of bright red strawberries and fresh
parsley propped in a cup. Or the warm wood of the kitchen
table. Color can't exist without light, and so I aim for light first,
and the color follows.

I've never invested a huge amount of money in my apartments, but I have invested a fair amount of attention. And I
think that it's that care that's made the most difference in the
places where we've lived. As I've said before, the specifics don't
matter. The real secret lies in making an effort to create something beautiful. Whatever you do, let it be intentional. Make
little shifts and changes designed to make you feel better about
the place that you call home.

In our apartments, I've often hung a rotating gallery wall of unframed bits and bobs in lieu of anything more formal. For one thing, framing is costly, but more importantly, I've found that my mood shifts and suddenly I want to take everything down and start fresh. Making a temporary gallery wall means I get to fill it with whatever's inspiring me in the moment.

Slow Design

The best decorating is done slowly. Slow allows for serendipity. Slow allows you to stumble upon the perfect dressers to match the headboard you lashed to the roof of your car. Slow allows you to invest in a table that was made by a woodworker in a tradition that you admire. It allows you to live without a light over the kitchen table until you find the perfect one. It requires patience, yes. But the reward of a home that reflects your personal style is usually worth the wait.

When you leaf through a catalog and cherry-pick the entirety of an apartment's furnishings in one sitting, some of the magic gets lost. More importantly, some of *you* gets lost.

Slow growth is often also the most sustainable choice. It means that your home might have the chance to be filled with something lovely and old. But it also likely means that you'll give yourself the time and space to search and save for a sustainable solution.

I know it's easy to get caught up in a cycle of more is more. Every day we're bombarded with advertisements, blog posts, magazine articles, books, and—yes—friends telling us about a new something-or-other that will improve our lives. Make something easier. Solve all of our problems. Make our homes more beautiful.

And feeling like there might be something that we could buy to make our work easier is tempting. But it's not always the path to thoughtful purchasing. My best advice is to slow down. Mull it over. Let it marinate. Choose whatever metaphor for taking your time that best works for you, and do it.

Consider the first trip to a big box store after a move to a new apartment. Do you know the one I mean? The one that you take while half of your things are still in boxes, but you find yourself stymied by the cabinet layout in the kitchen, or realizing that your old bath mat has gotten tattered and worn and a new one would just make you feel so much better about the slightly scummy mess left by the previous tenant. In the

I'm partial to hanging posters and photos with small metal clips like these. They usually cost less than a dollar at stationary stores, and over the years, I've even managed to snag a few special vintage ones for free.

mess of unpacking and figuring out what is going to go where, being able to cruise the aisles of a shiny bright store can feel like relief. I used to relish this kind of trip. In college, I'd make them after moving back into the dorms at the end of summer. After college, I'd accompany friends on their own mid-unpacking trips to get my fix between my own apartment moves. In a massive box store, it's possible to pick up a new bath mat, a shower caddy to fit the new shower head, and an over-door organizer for the pantry. While you're at it, you can get a few scented candles and pop a new throw pillow into the cart, because wouldn't it be just the thing to spruce the place up a little bit? A new bottle of shampoo is *just* what you need to feel at home in your new place. Plus, you need a new kind of tea—and what about those cookies?—and you think you might have spotted a side table that would work in your new bedroom. It's a slippery slope.

My first tip for slowing down? Avoid one-stop shopping. It's terribly convenient. But maybe it's too convenient. Even after years of committing myself to buying intentionally, I can still walk into a brightly lit box store and feel the urge to consume. Even when the shelves are lined with things that I

Good things happen to those who wait. James and I always loved vintage lab stools but we could never afford the ones we found in antique shops. After years of waiting, we found a pair of these beauties waiting for trash collection outside of a lab getting an update.

long ago decided that I wouldn't buy. I honestly think the best
trick is to avoid these kinds of stores altogether. Especially
after you've just moved someplace new. Especially when you're
feeling sad. Or hungry. Just pass on by. And once you're back
home? Step away from the computer. Being physically inside a
store is tempting because there's instant gratification. That new
side table is *in your hands* mere minutes after you've looked at it.
But online shopping can be just as problematic. With a click or
two of the mouse, you have made a whole slew of purchases that
you might not have made had the physical objects been in front
of you. I'm not suggesting that you not shop online—but shop
slowly. Bookmark the page for later. Pop that sucker on your
Pinterest fantasy board. Do whatever you need to do to take an
action, but wait for a moment or two before making the actual
purchase. If a week or two goes by and you still think you need
that thing, then by all means, it might be time to take the dive.
But I've found over and over again that simply delaying the purchase of something new negates my urgent need for it. It gives
me the time to remember that what I really want is a side table
with a *story*. And so I resume my wait for the perfect thing.

Sometimes decorating choices come down to necessity. In
our last apartment there was a gigantic floodlight outside our
only window. It meant that covering it up at night was crucial.
My window dressings have always been simple—cobbled
together in a homespun style. I used an old linen shower curtain,
a five-dollar length of iron purchased from a local iron shop, two
wrought-iron hooks, and a few safety pins to make a rod pocket.
Unconventional, yes. Cheap, yes. Ever-so-slightly wonky, yes.
But just what we needed.

In Providence, I hung curtains using just a little bit of string
and some nails, hammered into the edge of our wooden window
frames. I used pieces of white tablecloths. Understandably, you
might opt for a more finished look. When we made a small
changing area for our baby in our current apartment, I chose
to have purchased curtains re-hemmed by a local tailoring shop.
Twelve dollars later, I had custom-size curtains. A few more

In our house, curtain rods have always been fashioned from things we've found at the hardware store.

dollars later and I had a length of pipe and two pipe fittings to make a curtain rod out of plumbing equipment. My point is that you don't need to spend an enormous amount of money on custom window dressings to end up with a pleasant solution.

Maybe curtains aren't your problem. In our current apartment there's a backsplash that I don't really love. In between perfectly innocuous white tiles, the landlord added a strip of brightly colored mosaic tiles I don't much like. There are all kinds of approaches to this type of problem. I might have built a temporary plywood backsplash, or asked for permission to retile, or hung temporary tiles purchased for the occasion, but I didn't really want to invest in any of those options, so I cut strips of white adhesive paper and covered the offending tiles. It's a slightly funky solution, but it's one that was simple to execute and makes the space feel much more like something I would have chosen for myself.

Sometimes all of the catalog shopping and window gazing and blog reading can make me feel as if there's only one right way to approach decorating. But you can also get pretty darn far with a little bit of ingenuity and working with what you have, even if it's just a roll of white adhesive paper.

On Buying Previously Loved Furniture

The vast majority of the furniture in our home is made up of pieces that we either found on Craigslist or picked up off the street.

Save a few missteps in our early apartment years, our criteria has been pretty straightforward: real wood, simple design, nothing too bulky. With a little patience, a little luck, and a little searching, it's been fairly easy for us to find affordable furniture that we actually like.

We've often approached our furniture with the attitude of trade-ins. We've scoured yard sales and Craigslist postings and driven down questionable driveways to find just what we wanted. We've scrubbed and painted, and when we found something we liked even better, we've listed our own pieces and invited strangers into our home to relieve us of our castaways. James and I bought and sold a series of dressers before settling on the set that we still have today. Ditto kitchen table. Ditto kitchen chairs. The best part about furnishing an apartment with secondhand furniture is that the furniture doesn't lose value. Like buying a new car, as soon as you bring a piece of brand-new furniture into your home, its value diminishes. But an old table? One that works just right in your current apartment but that might not work to take with you when you go? You can likely sell it for the exact same amount that you bought it for.

To be sure, some of finding secondhand furniture is simply a question of being in the right place at the right time. Put another way: dumb luck.

Consider our bedroom furniture. I rescued our headboard from my parents' attic where it'd been locked up for decades after a staircase was changed and it could no longer fit down the stairs. It came down only after one of my sisters fell between the attic rafters, leaving a 10-year-old-size hole in my family's second floor ceiling that had to be replaced. (Don't worry: Only pride and plaster were seriously injured in the fall.)

James and I drove the rescued headboard from Connecticut to North Carolina on the roof of our car. We stopped on the side of the road to retie it. We got stuck in a rain storm with it still on the roof. But we made it back to our very empty apartment. In the weeks after we moved the headboard, we scanned Craigslist for the perfect dresser to accompany it. James found one—a monster of a dresser with chipping veneer and drawer pulls that looked like something out of Versailles, minus the gilding. We fit both of our clothes into it, but we continued searching. When we stumbled across a listing for two dressers with carvings that echoed almost exactly the primitive carvings on our headboard, we took a drive and snagged them—two dressers for $75. Lucky break. But like most lucky breaks, it was helped along by us being on the lookout in the first place.

At the risk of obsessively scanning Craigslist, if you're looking for something specific, you will want to look regularly. And keep your eyes open. We've found two tables and even more crates on neighbors' stoops. One sister found her own vintage headboard on the curb near her front door, cast off moments before by a moving neighbor. Keep your eyes peeled.

Trade out what you don't love. Every piece you find might not end up being a piece that you'll want to keep for the long haul. If you have nothing in the way of furniture and you need to furnish your home with the leftovers from your parents' attic, don't feel like this needs to be forever-furniture. Though it certainly could be.

Finally, enjoy it. Viewed in the right light, hunting for secondhand furniture is a magnificent treasure hunt. And the reward is certainly sweeter after a hunt. You'll not only have found a bookshelf or a desk, but a story, too.

Live With What You Love

I've mentioned that when James and I moved into our tiny apartment we had to make choices about what furniture came along with us. Even though we knew we'd leave behind some of it, we also resolved that we wouldn't just give everything up and start over. That decision meant that we retained

We've had to use our bedroom furniture in unconventional spaces in small apartments, but it's been a way for us to hold on to beloved dressers.

our personal sense of style, even if it wasn't always the most space-efficient choice. There was a wall in our tiny apartment where a tall dresser might have made more sense than a short one. A savvier apartment dweller might have chosen to forgo the dresser entirely and install a vertical wall unit instead. We surely would have had more floor space had we built ourselves a drop-down table. We might have been smarter to only squeeze stools around our table instead of four chairs.

But every decorating decision can't be made with practicality in mind. Choosing to keep most of our furniture means that we still have the pieces we most love today. In these cases, when it came to our gut checks, we chose love over efficiency. The romantic in me didn't want to part with the old dressers that we bought in North Carolina. And I didn't *have* to. I just needed to compromise. Yes to the dresser, no to efficient vertical storage. But here's the thing: We didn't really *need* efficient vertical storage. We'd pared down our belongings and committed to having less for the express purpose of being able to go without special convertible furniture and expensive storage solutions.

Bottom line: There have been more than a few cases when I've chosen to go for the romance. If you love something—and it's useful—you can make it work, whether it was built with maximum efficiency in mind or not.

Avoid Decorating Traps

A key for me to living with less is avoiding the trap of too many decorative elements. This isn't to suggest that a home needs to only follow the strict asceticism of a Puritan farmhouse, but it is to suggest that thinking twice before buying decorative items might be a good habit to practice, especially if the goal is simplicity.

Home goods stores line their shelves with decorative objects that they hope will line your shelves. The trouble with many of these mass-produced items is that this season's plastic

A decision to replace an old love seat with a vintage canvas cot and throw pillows has afforded us more room and flexibility in this space.

tray with a neon stripe becomes next season's plastic tray with a metallic stripe. A decorative doodad might provide the jaunty *oompf* that you think your living room shelf so badly needs, but it might just as well be an afterthought—an impulse purchase that gets made on the spot, without much thought about how it'll integrate with the rest of your home. Purchased to fill a decorative void, the object has limited sentimentality, which no doubt will impact the likelihood that it sticks around, or brings you joy, or does much of anything but collect dust.

Probably most important of all, much of this kind of decoration is not sustainably made. To keep price points down, stores mass-produce things like picture frames and vases and other bits that are easy to believe you need to buy every season. Like the fast-fashion clothing epidemic, there seems to be a similar schedule of big-box decorations being churned out in a manner that makes you feel as though your decorating choice is outdated nearly as soon as you bring it through the front door.

My own approach has been to add decorative pieces slowly, over time. I don't keep an enormous number of things in my home, and so I want each of them to really count. Sometimes those things have been a special purchase made while traveling. Or a favorite vintage item found among the rubble of a tag sale. Other times, I've set my sights on something made by an independent designer I admire and I've saved my pennies until I could afford to support the work. And in the meantime? There have been some sparsely populated shelves that I've filled with fresh flowers, or a favorite candle, or something else ephemeral.

Decorative Materials

Beyond passing my first test—do I love it—I try to keep in mind the materials used to make the objects in my home, and this is even true of larger items like furniture. This is an imperfect list, but here are a few things that I look out for when decorating:

Wood: Made of something that was once a living, breathing organism in its own right, part of wooden furniture's appeal for me is its warmth. Solid wood furniture is sturdy and more likely to last through moves and children and general wear and tear. More importantly, furniture made from real wood has typically not been constructed with a lot of glue or other adhesives that can off-gas into the indoor air.

Finishes, Paints, and Stains: When possible, I opt for natural finishes like beeswax and tung oil over synthetic finishes like polyurethane, which can off-gas chemicals like formaldehyde into your home. When I've painted furniture, I've chosen zero-VOC paint and made sure to paint in a well-ventilated area.

Upholstery & Stuffing: I always look for upholstered furniture that's been stuffed using cotton and wool instead of the more common polyurethane foam. In an effort to reduce fire risk, the highly flammable foam is saturated with chemical flame retardants that have been linked to cancer, neurological deficits, developmental problems, and impaired fertility.[1]

Simple Arrangements

My favorite kind of arrangements for putting around the house are the sort that look freshly plucked from the garden. Of course, living in the middle of the city without a garden to call my own, I still satisfy the urge by buying bunches of flowers that have a garden look, even if they weren't harvested by me:

Coneflowers
Daisies
Heather
Hydrangea
Lilacs
Queen Anne's Lace
Waxflowers

Sometimes, just adding a touch of greenery is all you need to make a bright statement. Some of my favorite filler plants that still look sweet all by themselves:

Bells of Ireland
Bupleurum
Eucalyptus
Grasses
Mint
Scented Geranium

Magic in a Can of White Paint

In apartment after apartment that I've lived in, I've experienced the magic of a quart—or gallon—of white paint. When you rent—and even if you don't—it can be nice to feel as if you're starting fresh. A yucky closet breathes new life with a coat of fresh paint. A silvery pipe disappears with a quick paint job. When I move into a new apartment, I buy at least a quart of zero-VOC white paint to freshen the place up.

Here's a partial list of things that I've repainted to great effect:
Cabinet shelves
Exposed pipes
Hooks
Interior doors
Interiors of closets
Medicine cabinets
Radiators
Undersides of sinks
Windowsills

Paint Safety

VOC stands for volatile organic compounds. Put simply, they're chemicals that are emitted as gases from both solids (glues and adhesives used in furnishings) and liquids (paints, lacquers, cleaning supplies), and they have both short-term and long-term adverse health effects ranging from mild runny noses and eye irritation to cancer. These air pollutants tend to be two to five times higher inside than outside.[2] While studies show that opening windows and introducing houseplants to a home can reduce VOCs in the air, avoiding them in the first place might be worth considering.

And caveat for fellow vintage-furniture hunters: furniture painted before the 1977 ban will likely contain lead paint. If you have a painted antique item in your home—and especially if you have small children—you'd be wise to have the table tested for lead. The alligator-scale crackle might make for a pretty picture, but lead is highly toxic and beauty shouldn't come at the expense of your health.

05:

Bath & Beauty

05:

Bath & Beauty

*"There must be quite
a few things that a hot
bath won't cure, but
I don't know many
of them."*
—Sylvia Plath

First: a little bit about the bathroom itself. I like to approach my own bathroom—cracked tile and peeling bathtub paint and all—with the attitude of creating an oasis. Like other corners of my home, I want it to be a space that's easy to clean and that fosters a feeling of calm.

Picture a spa. For myself, I'm conjuring images cobbled together from magazine spreads and movies, since I have to admit that in my thirty years I've never been to a spa (though I'm not giving up hope). In the spa of my imagination—and likely yours, too—I see white walls, a lit candle, perhaps a well-placed wooden bath mat, a stack of fresh, white towels. It's not a cluttered space. There's no countertop overflowing with products. There's no cabinet stuffed to overflowing with gadgets. There's no fuzzy toilet seat cover. Or stack of extra tissue boxes. Or toothpaste tube left open on the counter. It's a spare space.

Even if your bathroom is decked out in pink and white tiles—a Pepto-Bismol color I've seen in many a New York apartment—you can create the same sense of calm. My current bathroom was spared the Pepto-Bismol pink. It got the butter yellow instead, as well as what you might call a speckled, Mondrian-style floor, if Mondrian used speckles and lacked artistic vision. Still, it's spare. I have two small lidded baskets propped on the floor for holding supplies that I don't want to see displayed—extra soap, a hair dryer, thermometers, etc. I have a small cup for keeping our toothbrushes. I keep a vintage tray on the back of my toilet where I keep my toiletry kit and an array of helpful bath supplies like Q-tips. When I want to feel as if I'm vacationing somewhere far away, I close the door, light a candle, pour a bit of sweet almond oil into the tub, knock a few drops of lavender essential oil on top of that, throw in a handful of Epsom salts, and ignore the fact that the paint on the bathtub is peeling away while I take a bath. It's not perfect, but it is peaceful.

One of my favorite ways to visually simplify my bathroom is to decant. From shampoo to Q tips to throat lozenges, just about everything comes out of the packaging that it came in and gets put in a simple glass bottle or jar. For me, the visual clutter

of labels on products creates a feeling of disorder, but removed from their packaging, the same item feels useful and purposeful and like something that belongs to me. I think it's these little acts of care that end up making the biggest difference in a space. The tiny pink glass that I reserve for Q-tips was found in my parents' backyard. The jam jar where I keep cotton rounds is a flea market find from a winter wander with James. Even in my bathroom, I like for the items in my space to have a story.

We started using linen bath towels in our tiny apartment because they dry super quickly. In such a tiny space, we risked having the whole apartment smell like wet towel, and wet towels smell like mildew, if we didn't choose a quick-drying option. Happily, the linen towels were also attractive—which was helpful when the only place to hang them was from hooks on a door that opened into our one-room apartment.

But what about the products themselves? The toothpaste and shampoo and moisturizers and razors, and everything else that can have a way of exploding in a bathroom?

I was once directed to the bathroom of a new friend and was met with a room that looked like a ransacked pharmacy. Her large vanity was filled with half-used bottles of lotions, sunscreens, toners, and hair sprays. In almost every case there were multiples—a second and third variation of products designed to do nearly the identical thing. I think part of this is a result of too many choices. Each new product that we encounter makes a slightly different claim than the last, leaving us believing that trying something new will solve the problem. If we find a shampoo to be lackluster, there are thirty other options waiting for us in the store the next time we go. But beyond just fighting the temptation to try something new, I think part of the problem with accumulation lies in the volume within our homes already. When a countertop is already crowded with choices, we hardly notice adding something new to the mix. When a shower has a caddy stuffed to brimming with half-used shampoos, we might not think twice about cramming in another. Too often, cosmetic cabinets and makeup bags and even the side of the tub become repositories for half-used, little-loved products. And like I said in the chapter about decluttering, the more that we allow the unused stuff to pile up, the more it grows. There's power in the act of cleaning out what we're not using. Once you make sure that everything in your bathroom is getting *used*, you'll be less likely to add something new. In fact, adding something new becomes a special treat.

Not to get too saccharine about it, but for me, using up the last sliver of bar soap and then getting to unwrap a fresh one is, well, joyful. I love peeling off the paper wrapper, or untying a ribbon, and placing a fresh bar of soap in the shower. It's like a tiny gift. I love the feeling of rubbing the still-hard edges of the soap between my hands as the soap gets wet for the first time. Developing a ritual of joy around something as positively mundane as a bar of soap? For me this is the joy that gets lost in the shuffle if we're not careful. When our lives are crowded with endless supplies of stuff, we lose the ability to get excited about something new.

Apart from making sure that I'm actually using up what I'm keeping in the bathroom, or busying myself by becoming ecstatic over a new bar of soap, I have another secret for barring from entry too much bathroom clutter. And largely it's a kind of clutter that you can't even see at first pass, but that's veritably stuffed into cosmetics and bath products. I'm talking about the actual *ingredients*. After all, more troubling than my new friend's messy countertop was the complexity of what was inside the stuff cluttering it. The beauty industry would have us believe that each of us has problem skin. That somehow, our body's largest organ was conspiring against us to give us oily, patchy, itchy, troublesome skin that's impossible to treat and impossible to love. In reality, it's safe to assume that at least some of the oily, patchy itchiness is coming as a result of what we're putting on our skin. Same goes for our hair and nails.

I can't remember the first time that I heard about parabens. Or sodium laureth sulfate. Or any of the many chemicals that find their way, mostly unregulated, into our skincare

I like trying a new soap
each time we run out, but
my favorites are simple,
cold-pressed bar soaps
made from coconut and
olive oils.

routines. But once I *had* heard about them, I couldn't *unhear* it.
There are petroleum by-products contaminated with carcinogens in our lip balm and moisturizers. There are tiny beads of
plastic in our exfoliating face washes—and eventually in our
oceans. There are phthalates—linked to cancer and hormone
disruption—in our shampoos and cosmetics. There's lead in
our hair dye and asbestos in our talcum powder. We've made
a mess out of trying to look good.

I spent several years wringing my hands in the aisles of
drugstores, unsure of which products I would feel comfortable
putting on my skin. But eventually I got tired of picking up
a bottle of shampoo, or moisturizer, or deodorant and being
unable to decipher the ingredient list. I'd resolve to try something, only to spot an ingredient I wasn't familiar with. I'd
try to remember which kind of paraben was the bad kind
of paraben. Or were they all bad? I'd try to remember what
the Environmental Working Group's Skin Deep Cosmetics
Database had said about phenoxyethanol—it *sounded* bad, but
was it bad? ("It's only okay" is probably the best answer.) But
ultimately I decided that I would go in mostly for products
that didn't need to be decoded in the first place. Making sure
I could understand the ingredient list of a product right off the
bat has been one of the simplest ways that I could tell if it was
something that I wanted to put on my body.

One caveat for this approach: The International
Nomenclature of Cosmetic Ingredients (INCI) is a global
standard for writing ingredients so that they can be universally
understood. This means that instead of using common names
like shea butter when listing ingredients, the Latin names get
used. Which means that you see things like *Butyrospermum
parkii.* Unless you're fluent in Latin, or a nineteenth-century
botanist, you might think you've stumbled upon dubious ingredients when really you're just looking at shea butter. Happily,
the common name is often included in parentheses on these
kinds of products, so I've found that as long as I read carefully
I can usually understand what I'm about to rub into my skin.

I won't make any claims to being entirely untainted. I've had a lot of trouble finding a natural shampoo that renders my hair anything that feels close to clean. I've tried to go without shampooing. I've used straight-up castile soap. I've tried to trick myself into believing that a coconut shampoo with a name that plays on the word *organic* couldn't be all bad. I've found a better coconut shampoo that's still not perfect. One hundred percent pure products are hard to come by. I've made a few allowances for products that aren't exactly good enough to eat. All of this is to say that the point is to try your best.

The oil-based moisturizer that I put on my face each morning is produced in small batches by modern-day apothecaries. The facial oil has eight ingredients, all of which I can spell without looking and all of which actually *mean* something to me. They are things that come from plants without too many steps from earth to bottle.

The cream deodorants that I've used have similarly familiar ingredients: shea butter, baking soda, arrowroot powder, and essential oils. I've even mixed up a batch of my own—admittedly not-quite-as-effective—deodorant in my own kitchen. No goggles or rubber gloves required.

Good for Your Baby, Good for You

I can't begin to count the number of times that I've heard parents talk about how they're on the lookout for safe products for their babies, but that they themselves are a "lost cause." You are not a lost cause. And if you're wearing it, your baby is, too. That's the thing with creams and lotions and scents: They don't stay put. They get absorbed and wafted and generally spread around. So I try my best to get the whole household on pretty much the same products. Simpler, better for all of us, much less clutter in the bathroom.

Do-It-Yourself Beauty

Even more satisfying than finding the perfect product to buy is putting your own kitchen to work. The result might not be the perfectly concocted creation of an apothecary, but it will be refreshing, affordable, and effective. I've loved using books like Cold Spring Apothecary's *The Home Apothecary* and Rosemary Gladstar's *Herbs for Natural Beauty* to play with different at-home treatments and do-it-yourself beauty remedies. Here's a list of what I keep on hand to play with at home:

I always look for raw honey that hasn't been heavily heated or filtered.

Sweet Almond Oil: A mostly fragrance-free, mild oil that's excellent to use as a carrier oil for essential oils or all on its own. An emollient that softens and soothes skin, it's also helpful in removing eye makeup.

Epsom Salts: Fragrance-free natural mineral salt full of magnesium and sulfates. Used to soften skin and relax sore muscles. Good for a foot soak or full-body de-stressing bath.

Coconut Oil: Helpful for all manner of beauty and cleaning (and cooking!) recipes, we always have a large jar of coconut oil in our cabinet.

Apple Cider Vinegar: A splash of diluted apple cider vinegar on a wet washcloth can work wonders as a face toner. (I'm still working on loving it for my hair.) A bottle full can be poured over herbs to make a spicy herbal tonic. A tablespoon or two works for a delicious salad dressing.

Beeswax: When you want to get a little more crafty, pure beeswax cakes can be used to make lotions, lip balms, and hand salves, not to mention a salve for your wooden cutting boards and spoons.

Dried herbs: I have an old tea tin that I keep filled with dried flowers: calendula, rose petals, and lavender for slipping into bath soaks and home remedies.

Honey: Good for sore throats, homemade herbal syrups, a simple late-night kitchen mask—you name it. I always keep a big tub on hand.

Essential Oils: Essential oils are highly concentrated extractions made from flowers, fruits, leaves, roots, and trees and they're a mainstay in our house for cleaning and personal care. When shopping for your own, look for 100 percent essential oils sold by reputable organic vendors and use with care. Here are ten of my favorites:

- Chamomile (*Matricaria recutita*): Sweet, herbal scent. Calming, antibacterial, and antifungal.
- Eucalyptus (*Eucalyptus globulus*): Cooling scent. Antiseptic, antifungal, and deodorizing.
- Grapefruit (*Citrus paradisi*): Bright citrus scent. Mood-lifting.
- Lavender (*Lavandula officinalis*): Floral scent. One of the most versatile essential oils. Calming effect on mood and healing properties for skin conditions.
- Lemon (*Citrus limonum*): Refreshing citrus scent. Used for disinfecting, deodorizing, and lifting spirits.
- Peppermint (*Menta piperita*): Clean, menthol scent. Antiseptic.
- Rose Geranium (*Pelargonium graveolens*): Sweet, flowery scent. Much more affordable than rose otto or rose absolute. Excellent for all skin types.
- Sweet Orange (*Citrus sinensis*): Bright, refreshing scent. Calming.
- Tea Tree (*Melaleuca alternifolia*): Medicinal, herbal scent. Antibiotic, antiseptic, antibacterial, and antifungal.
- Vetiver (*Vetiveria zizanioides*): Woodsy scent. Eases anxiety. Relieves stress and achy muscles.

Uplifting Sugar Scrub

One of my favorite at-home treatments that's also incredibly easy to make is a basic exfoliating sugar scrub: brown sugar mixed with coconut oil and scented with essential oils that you can change up depending on your mood and the season. You can stir up a batch in a just a few minutes, and the result is a moisturizing, exfoliating scrub that smells wonderful.

2/3 cup (140 g) coconut oil
1 cup (220 g) brown sugar
5 drops sweet orange oil
(sub most any
essential oil to suit
your mood!)

Blend coconut oil (warmed to room temp if solid), brown sugar, and essential oil in a glass jar. Use in the shower for an invigorating scrub.

06:

Getting Dressed

06:

Getting Dressed

"Vain trifles as they seem, clothes have, they say, more important offices than to merely keep us warm. They change our view of the world and the world's view of us."
—Virginia Woolf

I've written in broad strokes about decluttering a home. But the things that we wear—or, more precisely, the things that we don't wear—are often the biggest cause of clutter. Inside our dresser drawers and crammed into closets and lurking under our beds is often a pile of clothing that we couldn't begin to wear, let alone remember.

Before we can begin to talk about how to build a wardrobe, it's necessary to think about paring down. In the same way that the clutter of everyday life can make a home feel chaotic, an overstuffed closet renders one of the first tasks of the morning—getting dressed—a stressful rather than peaceful affair.

My utterly unscientific poll has me believing that just about everyone I know has a closet full to brimming with clothes that they can't, or wouldn't, or otherwise don't want to wear. In our quest to feel comfortable or look beautiful, if not merely presentable, we accumulate a quantity of clothes that finish by making the dressing process more complicated, not less.

We can blame ourselves for bad habits, but we can also blame a clothing industry that has increasingly shifted gears in an effort to produce a constant, never-ending stream of new clothes—cheaply. In the scheme of things, this is a fairly new phenomenon. Historically, fashion labels produced just two main collections—spring/summer and fall/winter—and major department stores had just four main selling seasons. But as department stores have been replaced by enormous fast-fashion chains, the choices on offer are constantly turning over. In her book *Overdressed*, Elizabeth Cline writes, "To an increasing degree, the look on display in clothing stores is rapidly changing. What's in stores this week is no longer what will be there the next week. What's in style now is different from what will be in style next year."[1] And the result is that many people are *constantly* shopping. Cline quotes a 2008 trend study that shows that Americans buy an average of 64 new items of clothing each year. That means we're buying more than one new item of clothing each week.[2] It's no wonder that we're overwhelmed. So what do we do?

Start by taking a look at what you already have.

In my own home, I have a small three-drawer dresser and a half of a closet in which to store clothes. I'm a pretty discerning shopper and still, even in this small space, I've often felt that I have too much of what I don't want and not enough of what I do. As a first phase in the larger game of building a wardrobe of clothes that I actually like, I've developed a step-by-step approach for getting *rid* of clothes.

I go through all of my clothes at the end of each season. Unless there's something that quite obviously needs to go, I resist the urge to purge clothes out of season.

To begin, I make three piles:

Pile #1—Stay: This is the easiest pile to make. In this pile go the things that I really love and are still in wearable condition. These include clothes that I wear frequently and that I feel beautiful in, even if the item is just a well-fitting sweatshirt to wear to the grocery store. Also included: clothes that I wear infrequently but that are the very perfect thing for a special occasion. The goal, of course, is to have Pile #1 be the largest pile.

Pile #2—Go: These are the clothes that have got to go, no questions asked—they're worn out, unwearable, or loathsome. I go through this pile and divvy it up into two. In one pile go clothes that I can turn into rags (think: armpits stained beyond salvaging, unmendable rips or tears). In the other go clothes that have outlived their usefulness to me but which might make someone else happy. This includes clothes that no longer

Keeping my closet filled
only with clothes that
I love and wear has
made getting dressed
considerably easier.

I try to keep the inside
of my dressers as tidy as
the outside.

fit quite right, but it does not include clothes that are in truly bad shape. Sometimes, unfortunately, this pile includes clothes I never should have purchased. These get packed up into a bag and are either taken to a consignment shop or thrift store, depending on their condition.

Pile #3—Ponder: This is the toughest pile to wrangle, and for me it usually requires a revisit. This is the pile of unloved clothes that I know I don't wear regularly, but that I'm not quite ready to part with—anything I haven't worn lately and/ or feel ambivalent about. This might include a particularly pricey sweater that's turned out to also be unbearably itchy, or a pair of pants that aren't quite comfy but that I can cope with wearing during a dinner out as long as there are sweatpants on the other side of it. These go back into my drawer or closet if there's room, or they get zipped into a bag for me to revisit upon the arrival of the new season. When the season for wearing them rolls around again, I reconsider. Sometimes I take them directly to the thrift store, but sometimes absence has made the heart grow fonder and I'm reunited with a pair of jeans that become a favorite.

If any of the clothes in Pile #2 would fall into Pile #1 if they weren't otherwise worn out, I try to make a note. Did I just part with my favorite white T-shirt? If yes, was it one that I loved unconditionally but that I still managed to ruin? If yes, is it worth replacing? I try hard not to rush out to replace what I've given away. Getting comfortable with owning fewer clothes makes keeping an edited wardrobe possible in the first place.

Lest I oversimplify the task of donating unwanted clothes, I should also note that our fast-fashion problem has resulted in a thrift-store problem. Ten or fifteen years ago, browsing thrift stores meant a likelihood of taking home a real score: the perfect wool blazer, a pair of vintage leather boots, a few cotton ringer tees with charming small-town sports team insignias. Today, thrift stores are being weighed down by the detritus of bad choices. Cheap clothing made of synthetic fabrics are overwhelming donation centers. Donation centers themselves have a highly sophisticated purge system, set up to make sure that nothing that isn't being purchased sits around for too long. Once the clothes get taken off the racks, they're compressed into cubes, shipped off to larger repository, and often sent overseas, setting off still another chain of reactions in the receiving countries. To be clear, this doesn't mean that you shouldn't be donating the clothes. According to the Environmental Protection Agency, each year, Americans throw away—to landfills—12.7 million tons, or 68 pounds of textiles per person. The EPA estimates that 1.6 million tons of that could be recycled or reused. But as Elizabeth Cline is smart to point out in her book, we have the misconception that there's always someone else in our immediate vicinity who needs these clothes. We assuage our guilt about our bad clothing choices by assuring ourselves that someone in need is getting what we no longer want when that might not necessarily be true.[3] The bottom line: don't throw your unwanted clothes into the garbage, but don't expect that your neighbor is going to be the one wearing them, either. And then buy less.

Growing a Minimalist Wardrobe

After getting into the habit of getting rid of clothes, you need to find a strategy for adding them back in thoughtfully. Bombarded with choices, I admit that I've often felt overwhelmed by the process of shopping. Will I make the wrong choice and invest in something that I don't really like? Will the cycle of buy and purge continue without any lessons learned? To some extent, I think the answer is yes. Try as we might, it's hard to always make the right choice. We've all had the experience of trying on a shirt in a store only to get it home and decide that it's not as flattering or comfortable or wearable as imagined. And yet . . . we need to get dressed.

The words *growing* and *minimalist* might seem like strange bedfellows, but I've said before that I like to think of a minimalist wardrobe as being akin to a garden. You've got to pull out the mess and the weeds that are strangling the showstoppers and fill it back in with bits that will form a beautiful base and make your garden shine.

Choose a Color Palette

The most successful gardens start with a color palette. Maybe it's all silvery grasses mixed with blues or rich burgundies and deep greens. Maybe it's basic whites and blacks. Find a beautiful garden, and you'll also find a color palette. For me, the same goes for growing a minimalist wardrobe.

My palette is all blues and grays and whites with a few blacks and browns thrown in for good measure. Mostly these are colors that might be described as neutrals. For me, this has been the easiest way to have less, but this is not to say it's the only route to take. Maybe your color palette is red and yellow and blue with a smattering of green. Regardless of the specifics, if you're hoping to pare down your wardrobe, the easiest way I've found to do this is to find a collection of colors that you love and to commit to that palette.

Choosing clothes in a similar palette means that I can mix and match and know that one thing that I pull out of my drawer is bound to match the next thing. I like to think of my entire wardrobe in the way that I think of packing for a trip. Into my suitcase would go clothes selected to achieve the best possible mix-and-match traction. They'd be clothes that could be dressed up or dressed down. They'd be clothes that I enjoyed wearing.

This doesn't mean that a wardrobe might not have a few fabulous outliers. But the trick for me is to have a strong enough base to be able to welcome the oddballs.

Stock Basics for Layering

For a long time I felt like the word *basic* used as a noun was mere marketing fluff. But I've changed my tune and become a basics devotee.

Here's the idea: Build a small collection of simple clothes that can form the base of the majority of your outfits. The key is that these basics can either be worn separately or topped with other things to make them feel more special.

Once I started paying attention to my color palette I realized that the clothes I liked best were all either blue, gray, black, brown, or white, with a smattering of green and occasional red thrown in for good measure.

In my particular wardrobe, the clothes I love the most are comfortable, fairly androgynous in style, and simple in design—and my basics follow suit.

Before I started paying attention, I always had too many outliers. Over the past few years, I've been trying to home in on which basics can help me through the week, with the ultimate goal of having fewer clothes that I rarely wear and more clothes that can work in multiple scenarios. I've said goodbye to the random camisole with a little embellishment along the edge that I could wear with exactly one sweater and swapped it for a camisole that works with many sweaters.

You don't need to purge the entirety of your closet and invest in a new basics wardrobe in one fell swoop. The important thing is to start paying attention. In my own wardrobe, it's been a slow process of finding what works best and deciding to reinvest in something similar or to try something new. I've flagged certain things as in need of replacing, I've wish-listed other things that are nicer versions of what I already own. Along the way I've ruled out items as not being worth re-buying. The idea is to cultivate an attitude of thoughtfulness.

Slow Growth and Limiting Factors

In my life, I've had the best luck in building a thoughtful wardrobe by doing so slowly and with limiting factors. When I voluntarily limit the things I consume by self-imposing standards of construction or manufacturing or material, logic follows that I finish by consuming less.

Here are a few rules of thumb that I consider as I shop for clothes:

Evaluate Ethics: Faced with a list of all the things we're told to evaluate in order to determine the ethics of a garment, we can quickly throw up our hands and declare, "Never mind. I'll just run around naked, then."

While I'm quite sure that all of us are glorious sights to behold in the buff, I think it's reasonable that society at large might expect us to be clothed. And so I can only suggest that we allow ourselves the time to consider the where and the what and the who of how something has been made and try our best to make choices that harm fewer people and ransack fewer precious resources.

It's hard to tick every single box of what makes a perfectly ethical garment, but if you embrace shopping with a critical eye, chances are you'll come out ahead. Happily, many designers are establishing policies of transparency. If following the chain of supply for your average pair of cotton leggings seems like it would require more research than you're willing to invest, that's because it probably does. But you also have the choice to buy a pair of leggings from a company that openly discloses its process.

Question Quality: Cheap clothes rendered unwearable after the first wash quickly expose the affordability fallacy of fast fashion. But inexpensive clothes aren't the only problem. Clothes at a range of price points can have questionable construction or dubious origins. And how very disheartening it is to splurge on something only to find that it's been poorly made. So make like your fussy great-grandmother and run your hand along those seams. Try things on before buying them. Lift your arms and check to make sure the armholes are even. Hold T-shirts up to the light. Some of this is certainly trial and error, so consider buying just one blouse and seeing how it wears before deciding you need the whole rainbow.

Factor in Fabrics: I try hard to build my wardrobe with as many natural or naturally derived fabrics as possible. For me it's often a question of feel: I prefer a rich wool or soft cotton to a polyester blend. But there are also the considerations of breathability and wear and environmental impact. And of course, for every point there is a counterpoint. Cotton is a naturally occurring fiber that's breathable and fairly long-lasting, but conventional cotton is a crop that uses an enormous quantity of pesticides. I choose organic cotton and linen when I can because it's been gentler on the earth on its way to becoming wearable.

Forget Fads: For me the key to a minimalist wardrobe is to turn a blind eye to at least some of the seasonal fads. I'm not saying I haven't been a victim of fickle fashion. But terrible fashion choices of the past aside, I do find that the more I stick to simple, timeless looks, the more versatile my small wardrobe becomes.

Shop Small: An amazing result of the rich online community that I've found through blogging has been access to and discovery of small designers. Buoyed by the reach of their e-commerce, these designers are able to sell high-quality clothes direct to the consumer. I am endlessly impressed by these small business owners. A word to the wise: Small businesses don't always have the resources of larger outfits when it comes to

At the risk of appearing jingoistic, one of my measures for ethical fashion is the "made in the USA" label. In many cases, this means that workers are earning a living wage, working in safe conditions, and the company is contributing to the local economy. It's not a perfect measure, but it is a limiting factor to consider, stateside.

I use a simple muslin bag filled with moth-repellent herbs to keep my woolen clothes safe from moths.

I've never had a good space for keeping a large jewelry box, so I keep my everyday jewelry in a small white dish on my dresser and my more precious pieces zipped into a cloth sack.

returns and exchanges. Do your homework before splurging, and double-check measurements and return policies. When possible, try the garment on in person or seek the opinion of a friend or, say, blogger who has experience with the product.

Take Your Time: Just like for home goods, the best decisions are the mulled-over ones. Impulse buys account for 99 percent of the clothes I've allowed to take up space in my closet without getting enough back in return. If you're considering a purchase, or find yourself lusting after a large number of things, give yourself the space to mull them over. Identify things that you think you'd love to own and then let the idea marinate for a while before pulling out your wallet.

Wear Hand-Me-Downs: As a child, I was the lucky recipient of a nearly endless supply of secondhand clothes. Small for my age, I was almost always able to fit into the clothes that my closest friends were outgrowing. Their mothers would cart garbage bags of used and outgrown clothes to our house, and I would rifle through the piles, pulling out what I liked best. Somehow it didn't dawn on me to be embarrassed that I was wearing my classmates' castoffs.

This kind of sharing economy is definitely something to be encouraged. But it comes with a caveat: I've found that when things are given to us as gifts, it can be even more difficult to say no them. But a home overflowing with *other* people's discarded items is still a home overflowing. Give yourself permission to say no.

Take Care of Your Clothes: I don't darn my own socks, though what a skill that would be to boast about. But I do try to take care of my clothes. I hand-wash delicates. I hang much of what I wash to dry. I use a gentle, nontoxic detergent. I try to keep away moths and other critters who might have at my precious sweaters by packing winter garments away in a zipped bag and hanging cedar, lavender, and thyme in my closet. They keep the closet smelling good, too.

07:

Cooking & Entertaining

07:

Cooking & Entertaining

In a quest for a simplified life, mealtimes play the unique role of being both one of the easiest places to simplify and one of the most complex. Reduced to its simplest meaning, a meal is an opportunity to nourish and fuel our bodies and minds so that we can get on with the rest of our day. Viewed another way, a meal is an opportunity to rest and reflect, to invite friends and family around a table to share a common meal and stories from the day. To talk with each other.

But mealtimes can become stressful. In a day crowded with work and responsibilities, taking the time to prepare a meal can feel like a burden, or at least like a luxury that we don't have the time for. At the end of a long day, I'd often prefer to be cooked for. I'd love to lounge on a couch and read a good book while someone else chops and stews and braises nearby. Pour me a glass of wine; I'll keep up conversation—I'll even play sous chef and mince the garlic—but I'd happily hand the reins of planning to someone else. But since alas, alack, I don't always have the opportunity to be waited on hand and foot, it's a relief to have tried-and-true recipes to fall back on. It's encouraging to have a pantry—even a tiny one—stocked with foods that I know can be turned into something warming and nutritious or bright and refreshing.

I tend to rely on comforting foods that I've made before, but I also love a lunchtime ritual of browsing through favorite blogs or cookbooks for dinnertime inspiration. I look for recipes that look as if they'd be achievable without too much work on a busy weeknight.

This doesn't mean that I have something perfectly made-from-scratch every single night. I sometimes decide that the simple route is to order a pizza and toss together a green salad. There have been days when we've forgone the salad and scarfed down pizza all by itself. But there's also a fallacy in the amount of time that we perceive making dinner takes. In that landmark Los Angeles study of American families, researchers noticed two important trends around mealtimes. The first was the families tended to stockpile prepared foods that they could reach for come dinnertime—often preparing a different meal for each family member—and the second was that preparing those foods saved only a few minutes when compared with preparing a meal from scratch.

For me, more often than not, meal preparation is actually a blessed distraction. A moment when I can step away from

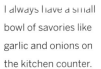

I always have a small bowl of savories like garlic and onions on the kitchen counter.

a computer screen and power down both literally and figuratively. Half of my writing gets done while chopping vegetables, which is to say: I churn the sentences over in my brain as I cut into a head of cauliflower. I allow my eyes to cross as I stare at pasta burbling on the stove. There are days when I begin the process of making dinner early just so that I feel the creative reset that comes with putting my hands to work and letting my brain go quiet. I'll hit a slump in the mid-afternoon, and I'll head to the fridge. I'll squat and balance on the balls of my feet, pulling out a bundle of kale or a bunch of carrots. I'll roll an onion in my hand, peeling off the paper skin and, like some

I find that letting what's looking good at the market guide my meal planning takes so much pressure off. Radishes looking fresh? Decision made.

kind of Pavlovian response, the act of cutting into it instantaneously calms my breathing.

But I don't always have the time for that kind of late-afternoon indulgence. There's child pick-up to do and deadlines to meet and a million other things that can seem more important than getting started. So even though I wax poetic about the joy of onion chopping, I'll offer a few practical tips as well.

Before I do, let me say that this is not intended to be a chapter that adds to the noise of advice and rules surrounding food. And to be clear: I'm not a professional chef or a nutritionist. In our house, we tend toward following the advice of wiser food writers. Michael Pollan's famous dictum "Eat food. Not too much. Mostly plants." is one that's pretty easy to adhere to, once you've gotten into practice. James and I share the responsibility for preparing our meals. We do our best to make simple, balanced, and nutritious meals comprised of real foods. I happen to be vegetarian. James happens to have a deathly allergy to potatoes. I really love dairy. He adores pasta. But our particular dietary restrictions or preferences don't much matter; it's the straightforward and affordable ritual of cooking at home that keeps our lives simple and our bellies full.

For me, simplifying mealtime is partially about keeping a list of basics in stock around the house and partially about letting what's good and fresh and easily available guide our meals.

Meal Planning

Meal planning is one of those simplifying tricks that sounds like more work than it's worth. It seems fussy. Worse, it sounds like a killjoy. When I think about meal planning, I see visions of spreadsheets and shopping lists. Where's the happy-go-lucky spontaneity when planning your week down to the foods that you'll consume?

But on the other hand, meal planning can offer a much-needed break from dinner-hour panic.

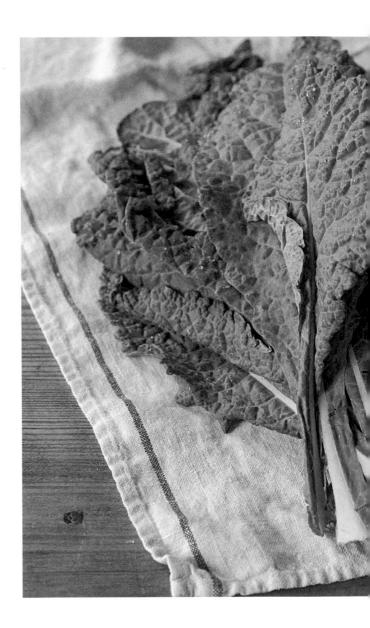

I find that keeping bowls of fruit out on the kitchen table means they actually get devoured instead of shriveling up in the fridge.

Spending five minutes deboning kale on a quiet weekend afternoon can keep me organized—and sane—in the juggle to put dinner on the table during the week.

For me, the best system for grocery shopping is one that allows for a bit of flexibility. The easiest way for me to keep a streamlined but hardworking kitchen is to rely partially on well-stocked staples and partially on goods picked up on a whim on my walk home.

James and I stop into our local grocery store on a near-daily basis. To be sure, this is partially a city convenience. When we lived in North Carolina, our beloved grocery store was miles away from our house and only reachable by car. We needed to be resourceful and plan ahead. Here, our nearest grocery store is three short blocks away. Three days a week there's a farmers' market just four blocks from our front door. Feeling moved by seeing a bunch of asparagus on my walk home and deciding on a whim to make an asparagus tart is a pleasure I relish.

But even if stopping into a grocery store on your walk home from work isn't something that fits into your daily routine, I think a combined system of structure and freedom might be a good one to try.

We've found it to be helpful to establish a framework for weeknight meals. We don't eat the same thing week in and week out, but we do tend to eat *similar* things. There might be pasta on Monday, stir-fry on Tuesday, salad on Wednesday, soup on Thursday, and sandwiches on Friday.

We certainly change up the order, we definitely change up the ingredients, but keeping a framework in mind helps with speedy grocery shopping.

Maybe most helpful of all toward maintaining sanity, we feed our daughter the same things that we feed ourselves. Save one emergency jar of prunes, we never bought prepared baby foods. But I didn't slave away at a stove boiling and pureeing either. Mostly, we experimented.

When Faye was just starting on solid foods, we'd make her a special bowl of extra-cooked oatmeal, or mashed up bananas—stuff we already had around the house but that received an extra layer of mushing to become palatable. As soon as she could manage—which was sooner than we'd even anticipated—she simply started to eat what we eat. To be sure, there have been moments when she hasn't seemed to like something that we've served. But we don't worry about it. After all, we can always try broccoli again another day.

There are lots of philosophies about feeding food to children, and we borrowed from what made sense to us. We spoon-fed Faye things like yogurt and lentils and applesauce. We let her feed herself things like chunks of avocado, and chickpeas, and squares of tofu. Slowly she'll learn how to hold her own fork and spoon—a stainless-steel set in miniature. We don't have plans to invest in a whole set of plastic dishes. Faye uses a tiny glass cup at dinner. She only dumps its contents in her lap every other time we sit down to eat. We're learning—and teaching—together.

Preparing Ahead of Time

In a habit that I've acquired while cooking in a tiny kitchen, I find it to be helpful to do at least a modicum of meal prep in one go at the beginning of the week. In a kitchen with limited counter space to spare, being able to optimize it during cooking is essential. An apartment-size refrigerator means we don't have a ton of room to stockpile foods, but having precut veggies or pre-boiled eggs or precooked rice could mean that during the actual dinner preparation on a given night, I have fewer dishes to crowd the sink. There's the added advantage of making sure that I put to use what I've purchased. Finding the time on a Saturday or Sunday to prep veggies purchased at the farmers' market, for instance, makes it so much more likely that I'll remember to use them during the week. And I admit to getting a buzz of satisfaction from keeping a tidy refrigerator that gets progressively emptier as the week hums along.

And of course there is a time savings. Hard-boiling eggs for a quick egg salad, scrubbing carrots, and washing and deboning kale are all things that I can do over the course of forty-five minutes on a weekend afternoon and the ten minutes that each task saves during the week can make dinner prep feel less daunting.

Buying in Bulk

I'm not talking about thirty-six rolls of toilet paper in one go. Turns out, it's not just the hard goods that we had to worry about in a tiny apartment. Finding room for the stuff that gets eaten was a challenge, too. Before they get used up, comestibles can take up an awful lot of room. Unless we wanted to share our couch with an oversize bag of basmati rice, we had to think carefully about what we brought home from the grocery store.

For the most part, we've solved our space issues by buying from the bulk section at our local independent grocery store. This approach has the triple advantage of allowing you to buy just as much as you need, leaving lots of unnecessary packaging out of the equation, and being more economical. Bonus: It might make you feel a special kinship with Laura Ingalls Wilder.

If you do a little searching, you can probably find a grocery store near you that purchases in bulk. Remember what I said about finding allies? The premise is simple: The grocery store buys a lot of one thing so that you don't have to. You can buy the amount of quinoa or rice or raisins that fits into whatever jar you have at home and never worry about finding space for awkwardly shaped boxes and bags. If you bring your own cloth produce bags, you reduce the amount of waste that you funnel to your nearby landfill or recycling center, too.

At home, I like to use mason jars for bulk storage. At around fifteen dollars for a pack of twelve (or no cost at all if you take the time to collect used ones), these glass jars are definitely the best bang for your buck. They come in lots of sizes, so there are options for things we might like to have more of, like sugar or flour, and things we might only have a few of, like dried apricots. In a kitchen with open shelving,

A sheet of muslin coated with beeswax, jojoba oil, and tree resin creates the tacky cloth called Bee's Wrap that will cling to a bowl like plastic wrap. Next step: learning to make our own.

Keeping staples on hand means that even on a night when we don't have time to think about dinner until we're already hungry, there's usually still something in the house to turn into a meal.

a basic mason jar is still pretty enough to look at that you won't mind keeping it out in the open.

Food Storage

Part of our efforts to reduce the amount of waste in our lives has meant taking a look at the ways that we store leftovers. Disposable options like plastic wrap and aluminum foil go straight to the landfill in most cases, so we've opted for lidded glass storage containers. Or we get creative: In a pinch, a dessert plate balanced on top of a mixing bowl does the trick to keep an extra portion of salad fresh for a day. The waxed paper wrapping from your butter can be used to cover the pastry dough you need to chill in the fridge. A recycled jelly jar can store an extra portion of soup as easily as Tupperware.

Of course, there are occasions when a bit of convenience is nice. We do keep a roll of parchment paper on hand for baking, and we sometimes dip into it to wrap up brownies to deliver to a friend or wrap up half an onion. We've also had great luck with a delightful product made in Vermont called Bee's Wrap.

Developing a Ritual

More than anything else, simplifying mealtime for us means simplifying the actual activity of mealtime. It means just eating, not eating and working. Not eating and scanning our phones. As I said in the introduction, life doesn't always feel simple. There's the possibility of a million distractions. Or excuses. Reasons why sitting down to a meal that's been intentionally prepared feels too challenging in the midst of a busy week. In our family, we have a weekly—at least—dinner with my sister and her family. In her tiny apartment or in ours, we gather to share a meal. If we're not hosting in our apartment, gathering for this meal means packing ourselves into a subway car and traveling under the East River. As we rumble along the train tracks, it's sometimes easy to think about the other things that we should be doing, like vacuuming, or finishing a blog post, or getting ahead on the week's grading. But the weekly dinner with my sister is so necessarily distracting. The way that it wrenches us out of our own life and catapults us into each other's is crucial. The joyful, raucous mess of it finishes by making us feel better. Improbably, the ratio of four adults to two babies sometimes means that fully two of us need to be engaged in the work of child-wrangling. Sometimes the conversation during meal prep gets interrupted by rollicking renditions of "Twinkle, Twinkle." Sometimes someone or another needs to sit on the floor and build a block tower for the express purpose of getting it knocked down—repeatedly. But we're together. We're eating. We're enjoying our food and most importantly, we're enjoying each other.

Entertaining

If you live in a tiny apartment and you'd like to maintain your sanity and still have friends for dinner, some advance planning, if not rigid rule abiding, can really help. But even in much larger spaces, a simplified approach to entertaining can mean optimal enjoyment for everyone involved. I think the best meals shared among friends consist of simple fare: one-pot meals, finger foods, dishes that can be prepared ahead of time. So many of the best comfort foods happen all in one dish: savory tarts, big pots of soup, pot-pies, lasagnas, a hearty main-course salad. They're guaranteed crowd pleasers and they require fewer dishes and serving utensils than more complicated meals. Even better, many of the best one-pot meals are actually improved if you leave ample time between preparation and serving: a soup that thickens over the course of an hour or two; a chili whose flavors meld over time; a tart that requires an hour in the oven and can be served at room temperature.

I often serve a savory tart for weekend gatherings. The process is simple, the result is filling and warming, and there are nearly endless variations, all equally delicious. Best of all, it's portable for picnics.

Regardless of what you serve, try your best to make at least a portion of it in advance of your guests' arrival. You'll leave yourself more time to enjoy your company and your guests less time to get underfoot. While your dinner cooks, take the time to set the table and do as much cleanup as possible. And what you can't get finished, move out of sight. It sounds preposterous, but when space is limited, you need to get creative. A dirty roasting pan stuck back in the oven (or into the bathtub) until you have a chance to clean it means that it's not hanging out in the open taking up space that you could use for something more fun.

The best gatherings are the simple ones that don't require much in the way of frills or fanfare. I've found that without much effort you can elevate the look of a simple gathering by following a few basic guidelines.

- Use serving dishes. It doesn't matter if they're large and formal or several small plates arranged in a cluster to mimic a larger platter. Just take everything out of its packaging from the store or travel and arrange it purposefully.

- Forget fancy. Wine glasses are a lovely luxury to have, but simple juice glasses work as well for serving wine. If you don't have the room or the budget to invest in stemmed glasses, choose a simple tumbler instead.
- Use the good napkins. Better yet, don't reserve any of your napkins for special occasions only. To avoid creating a lot of extra waste, I usually opt out of using disposable dinnerware, but if you're hosting more guests than you can accommodate with the cutlery and dishes that you have, go the simplest route possible and buy plain recycled paper options.
- Ask for help. If you know that your friend has just the right oversize salad bowl that you could use to serve your guests, ask to borrow it. Volunteer to pick it up yourself and return it with a thank-you. I've found that asking for a little help is the easiest way to avoid the waste of disposables or last-minute purchases of extras that you might not really need to own.
- Create a sideboard. Even in a tiny space, it's often possible to create a small sideboard out of something that you might not typically use for the purpose: the top of a washer or dryer, an open ironing board, a cleared-off bit of counter space.
- Add something green. A purposeful touch like a tiny bouquet of flowers or a sprig of fresh herbs in a small bottle or scattered on the tabletop makes a gathering feel festive.
- Serve herbal waters. Even if you keep your drinks selection basic, a pitcher or two of herb-and-fruit-filled waters instantly dresses up a table—and they're delicious.

08:

Cleaning

08:   Cleaning

To valorize do-it-yourself cleaning can certainly lead you into dangerous territory. Especially if you're a woman. Especially if you have things on your plate beyond scouring your home from top to bottom using nothing but a dash of baking soda and your own angel tears—which of course you do. Mine isn't a call to return to a life of drudgery, but it is a call to cast at least a discerning eye at some of the products that we're being sold in the name of cleaning and convenience. I won't recommend that we revisit all of the habits of our pioneering forebears, but I think there's something to be said for having a little bit of natural cleaning know-how up our proverbial sleeves; to hone the confidence to keep a house clean using ingredients that cost little and keep toxins out of your house at the same time.

Walk into any hardware store, grocery store, or pharmacy in the United States and you'll find a large aisle or two dedicated to household cleaning supplies. The options are many. Each of them claims to do a different thing. Specialized cleaners for toilet bowls, for tile, for fabrics, for glass, for furniture. Images of sparkly wine glasses, bouquets of flowers, and rainbows clamor. But when approached with simplicity in mind, some of the choices begin to fall away. And no surprise: A quick look at the ingredients lurking in those boxes would reveal that there's more inside than just sunshine and blue skies. But unlike in the cosmetics aisle, a glance at the ingredients lists isn't always possible. Getting a full list of ingredients used in household cleaners often involves making phone calls and conducting extensive research to find exactly what kind of chemical soup a company might have used. To consider: When the Toxic Substances Control Act was passed in 1976, it allowed 62,000 chemicals to stay on the market without testing. Since then, another 20,000 chemicals have been introduced. How many have been tested? Only about 200. How many regulated? Just 5.[1]

Put most simply: In the name of sparkling dishwashers and shining toilet bowls, we're flushing synthetic chemicals down our drains, swirling poison in our sinks, filling our homes with noxious fumes, and wreaking havoc on our hands and nasal passages—to say nothing of exposing ourselves to carcinogens. At the risk of sounding alarmist, I think it's safe to say

I try to keep all of my cleaning supplies limited to what can fit in one small wire basket.

I refill glass jars
with soaps and oils
for cleaning.

that we can do better. More than that, doing better can make our lives and our purchases less complicated, not more.

I like to think of cleaning know-how as a super dorky but very useful party trick. Red wine spills? Get out the salt! Spots on the stainless-steel range? Coconut oil. Roasting pan covered in a thick layer of muck? Porcelain sink stained? Baking soda to the rescue. Stinky cutting board? Half a lemon and some salt'll do you.

To be very clear: Cleaning is work, and it takes time and a bit of elbow grease, but it doesn't have to include an army of products, tools, and throwaway products. In part, this goes back to clutter.

A cabinet full of a different product for every possible cleaning dilemma you might face is a crowded cabinet. A cabinet stocked with a few cleaning basics is accessible and, dare I say, attractive.

What if you don't have time to make it yourself? I've been there. To be sure, there are cleaning products on the market that really work and that have been thoughtfully made without dangerous chemicals. I think the best approach goes back to finding allies—identifying the companies producing goods in a thoughtful, transparent manner.

Beautiful and Useful Cleaning Supplies

That old William Morris quote—"to have nothing in your house that you do not know to be useful, or believe to be beautiful"— gets batted around a lot but rarely followed. Or else it seems like a dictum that sounds nice in theory but for reasons of budget or disposition or general luck seems unattainable. But if we're going for aspirational, it seems like a nice thing to aspire to, even when it comes to cleaning supplies.

Look at your broom closet. (Or, if you live in a small space like me, look at the closet where you keep your broom—alongside all manner of other things, like clothes and coats and your shoe collection.) Chances are, there's a motley crew of cleaning accessories in that space. There might be the plastic broom you've had since college. A plastic dustpan with one corner that's cracked off. There might be an abandoned Swiffer, a package of dried-up sponges. If you're my dad, it's likely there's a stack of old, empty coffee cans just waiting for the moment they might become a vessel for paint or cooking grease. (It's thrifty, but cluttered.) Cleaning supplies aren't things that we tend to buy intentionally. They're things that we run to the hardware store to buy in a moment of panic because we realize that we've moved into a new apartment and the bathtub

In cleaning supplies and other things, I've found that the best designs are the ones that haven't been overly improved upon. Our dustpan and broom look like something that might have been used in our apartment a century ago.

desperately needs attention, or the toilet's clogged and there's no plunger, or the mirror's grimy and guests are coming over.

But I like to advocate for a different approach. Because the problem with so many of these cheap, ugly cleaning supplies isn't so much that they don't last, it's that they *do*. Those mismatched brushes and brooms and toilet bowl cleaners last and last. But if we treat even our most humble purchases with the same thoughtfulness that we might devote, say, to the purchase of a pair of shoes, we end up with more beautiful, more durable, more responsibly made goods. In a tiny apartment with limited space, I like to consider the beauty and utility of even everyday cleaning supplies. Unable to stash ugly plastic brooms or scrub brushes into a pantry or closet, I started a slow search to find long-lasting replacements for the plastic-handled accoutrements I'd been toting around since college. The sticking point being, of course, that throwing all formerly purchased scrubbers into the landfill only for the sake of beauty is, alas, also not a sustainable solution. But if you're just starting out—if, for instance, you're making your first-ever broom purchase—consider the long-term. Consider the beauty *and* the usefulness of the thing. Because the cheap broom will stick around, but it won't look pretty propped in the corner next to your bookshelf.

Wooden Brush Maintenance

After you take your time to gather together a beautiful collection of wooden brushes, you're going to want to take care of them. Keep in mind that all wooden brushes will show signs of wear after getting used regularly for scrubbing, but here are a few tips that I've found to increase their longevity:

Keep them out of water. I use a glass jar to hold my vegetable and bottle brushes while they're not in use. Keep the brushes brush-side-up so that they have time to air-dry.

Rinse them. Soap scum is the number one cause of a wooden (or any) brush getting gunked up. Give them a good rinse in hot water to make sure they're free of soap before drying.

Replace them: Your brushes *will* eventually need to be replaced.

Do-It-Yourself Cleaning Products

New to making your own cleaning solutions? Here are a few simple ways to get started:

Dish Soap: Adding essential oil to unscented castile soap can help take the drudgery out the ordeal. I like to add 10 drops of lavender oil and 10 drops of tea tree oil to 20 ounces (600 ml) of castile soap and then decant into a simple glass bottle with a pour spout for keeping on my countertop.

Glass Cleaner: Equal parts white vinegar and water combined with a few drops of citrus essential oil—I prefer orange or grapefruit—makes for a very easy glass cleaner. I use crumpled newspaper to wipe down the windows and keep them lint-free.

Wooden Floor Cleaner: Combine equal parts white vinegar and water with a hearty portion of peppermint oil—I use around 20 drops. Add the mixture to a spray bottle and spray as you mop. For a heavy-duty mopping job, add a small amount of castile soap to a bucket of warm water and add peppermint essential oil. Added bonus? Mice hate the smell, so you'll keep unwanted critters away if you live in a mouse-abundant city like New York. You may want to swap out peppermint for lavender if you've got pets or babies who could be sensitive to peppermint.

Greasy Pot Rescue: Caked-on dinner mess? Add a hearty dash of baking soda to a still-warm pot and add water. Let it sit while you eat and return to a much easier scrub job. If you forget to take the proactive approach, add the baking soda and a few cups of boiling water to a cooled pan. Allow it to sit while you tackle the other dishes and then wash as usual. (Also good for shining up nasty burner pans.)

Sink Cleaner: Pour ¼ cup (30 g) baking soda and ½ cup (120 ml) vinegar into your sink (I usually approximate both measurements), and add a few drops of your favorite fresh-scented essential oil. The mixture will create a satisfying sudsy foam like from elementary school science experiments. Wipe down with a sponge or brush and rinse with warm water. If there's residue left from the baking soda, rinse again with a bit of vinegar.

Sticky Residue Remover: As a habitual label-remover, I use this mixture constantly. Combine equal parts baking soda and coconut oil to make a thick paste. Apply mixture directly to the sticky residue you're hoping to remove and work at it with a warm cloth rag. The residue should come right off with a little elbow grease.

A Note About Safety

These natural cleaning solutions are free from unregulated neurotoxins and other things we don't like to talk about, but that doesn't mean that there wouldn't be consequences if they were digested. Anything you use to clean your home should be used with care and common sense. Remember: Essential oils contain VOCs, too. That's why you can smell them! They're not synthetic, they don't build up in our bodies, and they're not known carcinogens, but they are highly concentrated and should be used sparingly and in small doses. I use rubber gloves when I'm cleaning, even if I'm only using baking soda and vinegar. All of these products should be kept away from children.

Cleaning Essentials

I keep a basket full of cleaning supplies under my kitchen sink. Here's what I store inside:

White Vinegar: Plain old white distilled vinegar—like the kind you use to make pickles—is one of the most potent natural cleaners you can buy. Diluted in a solution of half water, half vinegar, it can be used as an all-purpose cleaner. Added to laundry, it works as a fabric softener (and a preventive or even corrective against mildewy towels). The smell dissipates when it's dry, so don't worry about your house smelling like a gherkin.

Baking Soda: Otherwise known as bicarbonate of soda. I'm not sure if there's anything that baking soda *can't* do. It works wonders for any kind of deodorizing. It also shines stainless steel like none other.

Lemon: I don't actually keep lemon under my sink; I keep it in my fridge, but it is a part of my larger cleaning arsenal. Good for deodorizing and cutting grease. I like to wash down my cutting boards with a half a lemon and a sprinkle of baking soda or salt.

Castile Soap: A basic, gentle, and plant-derived soap useful for all kinds of cleaning, castile soap is often sold in bulk at natural food stores and doesn't contain petroleum products like most dishwashing soaps. It's easy to scent using your own combination of essential oils.

Essential Oils: My favorite essential oils to use for cleaning are grapefruit, lavender, tea tree, sweet orange, and peppermint. *See page 123 for more essential oil uses.*

Coconut Oil: Touted for just about every use under the sun, I use coconut oil for everything from seasoning cast iron to removing sticker scum.

A list of cleaning supplies and ingredients that I've found to be helpful:

Rags: I like to use 100 percent cotton or linen rags cut into equal-sized squares. Well-loved jersey T-shirts or old flour-sack dishcloths make soft, inexpensive rags when they've outlived their original uses.

Vegetable Brush: I keep a classic wooden vegetable brush in a jar by my sink to wash dishes and scrub down my wooden cutting board.

Bottle Brushes: I keep two bottle brushes of different sizes to reach into difficult-to-reach spaces in glass vases and bottles.

Toilet Brush: What a thing to lust after, and yet. Finding a classic wooden toilet brush can be difficult to do, but not impossible. In our house, we've opted for a very simple metal canister brush from Ikea.

Newspaper: Helpful to use as a lint-free alternative to a cotton rag when cleaning glass windows and mirrors.

Glass Spray Bottle: It's useful to have a spray bottle on hand when making your own cleaning supplies. A classic glass

I think of a coir brush as a natural scrubby brush, minus the bright blue or yellow plastic parts.

We add soap to an old
whiskey bottle topped
with a pour spout to keep
by the kitchen sink.

vinegar bottle has the same size top that most conventional
spray bottles do, so you can use a plastic sprayer in a glass
bottle for homemade mixtures. Stainless-steel sprayers are also
a durable and lighter-weight alternative.

Coir Brushes: Made from coir—the fibers on the outer shell of
the coconut—these stiff-bristled brushes are incredibly sturdy.
We use ours for scouring our cast-iron skillets.

Vacuum Cleaner: Even in our smallest apartment, we kept
a full-size vacuum tucked in the closet. I've found smaller
vacuums to be ineffective and to break easily. Judging from the
number of these vacuums I've seen out on the sidewalk come
garbage day, I don't think I'm alone in this experience.

Metal Dustpan and Whisk Broom: When I don't want to
pull out the vacuum, I've found it to be helpful to have a
sturdy hand broom and dustpan. A metal dustpan with a clean,
straight edge makes for the easiest cleanup, and I'm partial to
a classic straw whisk broom.

Wet Mop: We don't wear our shoes in the apartment to cut
down on the amount of New York City street dirt that we track
in, but we've still found that a sponge mop and a biweekly
mopping is necessary to keep things sparkling, especially with a
crawling infant underfoot.

Bucket or Basin: We have an old enamel basin that we use
for mopping the floor. Galvanized steel also has a utilitarian
and rustic look that helps a basin look like decor when it's not
being used for sudsing the floor.

09:

Thriving

09:   Thriving

Lives are *always* more complicated than they appear. As someone who writes a blog where I share only a portion of what happens in a given day or week or year, I know firsthand this business of *realities*. There are beautiful moments that I share and beautiful moments that I bottle up to keep just for me. Same goes for sorrows. In any life, there's a daily influx of pain and growth and joy that happens regardless of the *stuff* or the space.

In our own lives, there have certainly been moments when the size of our space has felt like the challenge itself. Moments when I've felt stifled. Moments in our tiniest apartment when I wanted more of it just for me. Moments in our slightly larger apartments when I've wanted more of it just for me. Virginia Woolf was on to something, after all.

But in those moments, there are ways that I've found to unwind a bit. To thrive in spite of the close quarters, and maybe because of them.

This chapter focuses a little bit on simple ways that we can take care of ourselves and our homes. Things we can do to take back a little control, remember what really matters, and be gentle with ourselves at the same time.

Grow Something

Inside

Houseplants are having something of a heyday, but I don't think I'm alone in having some fusty associations with indoor plant collections. For years, I associated houseplants with tables upon tables of them at my grandmother's house. She kept the plants in a shadowy dining room that didn't get much light, so hers was a collection that could thrive without it; I mostly remember the African violets and snake plants. Despite the greenery, the scene was lugubrious.

But in the right quantities, a houseplant collection can be just what a home needs to feel alive. I keep a windowsill full of them and have one or two perched in other corners for an added dose of color.

Here's one thing I learned editing houseplant stories in my former job as an editor of a gardening website:

Forcing flowering tree branches is one of my favorite ways to make it through the last few weeks of winter and to welcome spring. You can successfully force most kinds of flowering tree branches with just a little bit of water and some patience. Some of my favorites are dogwood, forsythia, quince, cherry, and crab apple.

Adding a bit of color in the form of a houseplant can transform a room visually, but beyond looking pretty, houseplants work hard by producing life-giving oxygen and absorbing air-polluting toxins like benzene and formaldehyde. Just ask NASA.[1] I try to repot my plants every spring.

Herb starts are an affordable and practically foolproof way to fill an outdoor windowbox.

Houseplants require loving care. Just like you. The only houseplant that can be entirely neglected is a fake houseplant. If you have a dark apartment and fail to water your charge, or if you water faithfully but the pot is too small, your houseplant will suffer. I'm sorry to give bad news, but I can't see the advantage in sugar-coating this. The good news? Taking care of a houseplant might be just the sort of low-key hobby that you need. It doesn't take much time to whisper sweet words to your snake plant or give it a little water once a week. And for most plants, a sunny windowsill will do most of the work for you.

Outside

When I imagine my older self, I picture her having found a bit of land somewhere (no telling if that means in the back garden of a Brooklyn apartment building or on a hilltop in Maine). On that land I would grow simple things to eat, but there'd also be an abundance of flowers and herbs—those things that nourish a slightly softer side of the human spirit. There'd be milky oat tops and dainty chamomile. I'd grow five varieties of mint, because why not? There'd be a raspberry bush and a row of peppery nasturtium. I'd stake bean poles. And weave willow fences. I'd invite friends over for tisanes made from the herbs that I grew myself.

But until then, I satisfy the urge by growing a few little things in window boxes and trying my very hardest to remember to water them. My mint plants sometimes dry up. I've never had enough light in a city apartment to successfully grow lavender or rosemary or other light hogs. But I do my best to grow what I can. The planting itself is a simple act. On a spring morning each year I walk down to the farmers' market and buy up a few kitchen herb starts, then I stop at the hardware store for a bag of soil. I tuck my starts into weathered planters I've taken from apartment to apartment and hope for the best. It doesn't take much time and doesn't have quite the feeling of digging my hands into the cool earth and *really* gardening, but it's a ritual that I love to take part in each spring.

In our last apartment, I spent one spring working in the front garden. It was a neglected space, utterly overrun with

My enjoyment of tea is largely the enjoyment of the ritual—like that cup of morning coffee. Boiling water on the stove, pouring it over the tea leaves. Allowing the tea to steep before sipping on a warming beverage. In the early spring, I brew strong cups of tea with nettle in it as a way to stave off spring allergy attacks.

gooseneck loosestrife and English ivy and some kind of young tree that I never quite identified but that did its very best to regrow despite my best efforts to tame it. In March, when the earth was just beginning to thaw, I found crocuses shooting up from underneath a moldering foot or so of fallen leaves, and I couldn't just ignore them. Without exactly asking permission, I began to remove the gray, dusty leaves. In the afternoons after writing, I would go out and sit on my haunches and rip away ivy and thin the loosestrife. As I worked, my neighbors would greet me, delighted that someone had decided to take back what you might argue was the most neglected garden on the street. I was never able to completely transform the space. I didn't have the money to buy much plant-wise, and I didn't want to get too cheeky with my unsanctioned gardening, but what I did manage to do that spring transformed *me*. It got me out of my tiny apartment. It introduced me to my neighbors. When other things felt hard, weeding felt easy.

Practice Self-Care

In the same vein as tackling cleaning or planting a few things of your own, it's nice to have a few remedies for self-care tucked up your sleeve. You don't have to be an herbalist guru to dabble in the arts. There's lavender for keeping calm. Nettles for fighting allergies. Grapefruit for offering a bit of refreshment.

I don't eschew modern medicines, but I do relish the ability to calm my nerves with a hot pot of tea. Or clear my sinuses with a bit of eucalyptus. Or heal a bruise with a little calendula. Sometimes I tap into other people's expertise: The modern-day apothecaries blending together remedies that I can use when distilling my own essential oil feels about a million miles from things I'd reasonably be able to accomplish on a given day. (Every DIY enthusiast has her limits.) But on other days, I pull together a little something just for me.

Herbal Bath Soak

When I was in high school a psychic at a fun fair told me to take a weekly Epsom salt bath. I'm sure she told me other things, but the bath part stuck with me. Good for aches and pains and whatever else ails you, an Epsom salt bath is a simple solution for feeling good quickly. On busy days, I toss a handful or two of salt into the tub, then add a few drops of sweet almond oil and a few drops of a favorite essential oil. Given the chance, a bath can provide a reset. It's the actual time spent taking the bath that helps more than anything—the repose, the time to close my eyes.

On days when I have a little more time, I like to make an herbal bath soak.

What you need:

2 parts Epsom salt

1 part dried rose hips

1 part dried chamomile
    flowers

Small muslin pouch
    with drawstring

To make your own, combine the salt, rose hips, and chamomile flowers in a small muslin pouch. Tie it closed and crush the mixture between your hands. Tie your pouch to the faucet and let the warm bath-water run over it as it fills the tub. You can let the pouch float in the water while you soak, like an oversize tea bag.

Shower Melts

Maybe you don't like baths—maybe you prefer showers. Maybe you only have a shower! Add a little aromatherapy before a stressful morning or after a long day.

What you need:

Baking soda

Water

Sweet orange essential oil

Lavender essential oil

In a small bowl, pour a small amount of water into your baking soda, mixing slowly and adding more water until the mixture resembles wet sand. Spoon the mixture into small molds—I use metal pastry tins that I'd saved from a tea light project, but a silicone ice cube tray would also work well—and allow to dry completely, preferably overnight. To speed up the process, I bake mine in a 350° F (175° C) oven for twenty minutes. When dry, add 5 drops of sweet orange essential oil and 5 drops of lavender to each mold. Dot with a tiny sprinkling of dried flowers if you want your melts to look pretty. Store in an airtight jar. When you're ready to use them, toss the shower melt onto the floor of your shower and enjoy a refreshing steam. (You can use these same things in the bottom of a trash pail, the bottom of a diaper pail, the back of a refrigerator—or anywhere else you can imagine that you'd like to smell better.)

A pot of jasmine kept
on the windowsill means
a fragrant reward come
winter.

A single stem of tuberose
is all you need to fill a
room with its sweet smell.

Make It Smell Good

You know that phenomenon when you return home after some
time away and you can *smell* it for what feels like the first time.
It's a bizarre experience. And what a funny thing: to smell and
not smell at the same moment. I always want that smell to be a
good one. Clearly, I'm not alone. There's an entire industry built
around home fragrance. Unfortunately, a lot of those fragrances
are made of ingredients that might be questionable. Fragrance
is on the list of sneaky little things that are more complicated
than they appear. Anecdotally: Most synthetic fragrances
give me a headache and make my sinuses hurt. To avoid the
unknowable (and headaches), I like taking a simpler approach
and fill my house with things that smell good naturally. To be
sure, there are some natural fragrances that can be as potent as
anything synthetic and just as likely to make my eyes smart.
Every spring I buy a bunch of hyacinths, and every spring

I have to open the windows and air the place out afterward. Talk about a headache.

I prefer subtle scents that make a space feel fresh or cozy depending on the season but that aren't quite as overpowering. In the fall and winter, a pot simmering on the stove is the perfect way to cozy up a space. I keep a little enamel pot for the purpose. In the fall, I simmer warming scents like apple, cloves, cinnamon, and allspice. In the mid-winter I might brighten things up with juniper berries, lemon rind, and rosemary. In warmer weather, a stem or two of a delicious-smelling flower is enough to fill a house. I like: jasmine, tuberose, lilac, and hyacinth.

Explore

After you do the work of making your home a sanctuary, get yourself out of it again.

Get outside. Go to museums. Take a walk through a different park. Read the Sunday paper on a park bench. Go to a flea market. Find a poetry reading. Meet a friend for a beer. Get a library card. Walk home from work. Whatever you do, get *out* of your apartment.

New York City is a city of extremes. The winters are very cold, and the summers are very hot. The fall and spring are utterly glorious and terribly fleeting. But regardless of whatever Arctic blast or heat wave we're enduring, I do my very best to spend as much time out of the apartment as possible. Sometimes that means packing a picnic and toting it to your local park, and sometimes that means hatching plans for adventures farther from home. It means trading your favorite blanket for a sleeping bag and the comfort of your bedroom for the exhilaration of sleeping under the stars.

As much as I believe in the hard work of homemaking, I believe in the art of home unmaking, too. In shaking up routines and in exploring the world beyond our daily haunts.

Picnic Essentials

Enjoying a picnic in the park is the perfect antidote to a stressful workday. We have an old basket that I found at a thrift shop and that we fill with a hearty salad, a slab of cheese, and crusty bread. When we're feeling especially busy, we'll fill it with banh mi from the local Thai sandwich shop and call that a picnic. It honestly doesn't matter much what we're eating, as long as we're outside in that golden hour when the sun is setting.

Picnic supplies we keep ready for impromptu meals outside:

Blanket/Tablecloth: For picnics in the grass, I like using a lightweight tapestry that's not much thicker than a bedsheet and easy to walk down to the park. When we opt to use a picnic table in the park, I always bring a small linen tablecloth. It makes all the difference in enjoying a meal in a public space, and it's easy to shake free of crumbs and toss in the laundry afterward.

Cutlery: If you're worried about toting your forks and knives to the park where they might get lost, consider buying a few extras inexpensively at a thrift store and keeping them stored in your basket between picnics.

Cutting board: A super-thin wooden cutting board sounds a little extravagant for a picnic, but we find that it's just the thing to elevate the setup a bit (and help prepare the picnic without too much struggle).

Foldable knife: A trusty foldable Opinel knife is always a good idea. From cheese to bread to cuts of salami, this knife can handle just about anything.

Backpack: Now that we have a baby in the mix, we've found packing a small backpack with lightweight enamel plates and a water bottle makes picnicking decidedly easier.

Picnic basket: I love the look of classic picnic baskets, but they're also really useful for keeping foods flat in transport and having a little portable serving area once you've arrived. Keep the heaviest stuff out of the basket and put in your backpack.

More Than White-Tiled Walls

Channel the nuns.

Or Fräulein Maria.

My point is: Have less—don't worry about the bathroom tile.

Remember that scene in *The Sound of Music* when Maria skips down the poplar-lined lane, swinging her one measly carpetbag in one hand and her guitar case in the other, belting her little heart out? You know it. Maybe you've even reenacted it. No? Only me?

Eleven years ago, when my sister Cait had just graduated from college and I was 19 and still smack in the middle of it, we took off for a two-week backpacking trip to Italy. I had managed to get myself a paying internship for the summer, and so she convinced me that the proper thing to do in advance of the start date was to empty my paltry bank account and book a ticket to Italy. We flew on a two-for-one deal on Swissair. I took many blurry photographs of the Alps with my film camera and relished sips of ginger ale mid-flight.

We ate pasta every single day of our visit. A Spanish soldier fell in love with Cait on the train ride to Siena. Other train rides got canceled, inexplicably, at the last moment, and we shrugged and hoisted our packs and took buses instead. I dirtied my feet wearing an old pair of Birkenstocks before they were trendy and then let the salty Mediterranean scrub them clean in Corniglia. We swore that one day we'd both honeymoon in Capri. We had an explosive fight on the Spanish Steps in Rome. I remained mute while Cait stumbled through her Italian in city after city, until—finally—she forced me to ask, "Which way to the Leaning Tower?" in Pisa. In Italian. I stammered through "*Dove*" before someone took pity on me. We ordered drinks at outdoor tables and wolfed down the free peanuts while shooing away the ever-present pigeons with our hats.

It was the first time that I'd left the comfort of my stuff to find the wider world on my own. Of course being with your big sister is nothing like being alone, but the point is that we were free, with only our backpacks to weigh us down.

We made our way from city to city, staying in grimy hostels and pristine convents. Yes, convents. There were curfews and starchy bed linens on twin mattresses. The only decoration was a cross on the wall and a bad painting of one or another saint. In our final hotel, our bag of carefully selected gifts for friends and family back home was either stolen or tossed down the garbage chute, we never knew which. We cried, and then we returned home empty-handed, our stories the only souvenirs we had to offer.

I'm not suggesting that the only key to happiness is giving up all of your worldly possessions and strapping on a backpack. Though it certainly seemed to work for Elizabeth Gilbert and Cheryl Strayed, not to mention all those saints.

I *am* suggesting that when I think back to times in my life when I have felt truly happy, calm, invigorated, at peace . . . they've been moments like these. Times when I had a bag full of clothes to wear, a roof over my head, food in my belly, but not so much at all in terms of stuff. In fact, if it weren't for a handful of photos, I don't think I'd remember what I wore or what I toted with me to Italy that summer. I *do* remember, vividly, the most delicious pint of strawberries I've ever tasted, and the feeling of the sun on the cobblestone *Piazza del Campo* in Siena, and the old lady scolding me in Italian to cover my shoulders as I waited for the pope to peek out of the Vatican. All moments I didn't take a single photo of and couldn't take with me when I boarded for home. Something about the lack of physical burdens freed me up to take in—and hold on to— the lived experience itself.

Here's the crutch: I genuinely like stuff. I appreciate good design. I enjoy keeping a beautiful home filled with beautiful things. Not lots of things. Nice things. You understand. And there are actual moments when it can feel as if my windowless, yellow bathroom with the missing floor tiles, the peeling tub, and the gigantic, grody mirror is the thing between me and happiness. That if only my bathroom were tiled white with a claw-foot tub and a spotless shower curtain, everything in the world would be right.

Here's a pact to remember to swing our metaphorical leather valises with gusto, à la Maria. To enjoy the strawberries and forget the gifts. To release the burden of the homes we live in and look for happiness elsewhere. After all, we are more than the sum of our possessions; we are more than white-tiled walls.

NOTES

Chapter 01: Decluttering

[1] Jeanne E. Arnold et al., *Life at Home in the Twenty-First Century: 32 Families Open Their Doors* (Los Angeles: Costen Institute of Archaeology Press, 2012), 23.

[2] Arnold et al., *Life at Home in the Twenty-First Century: 32 Families Open Their Doors*, 25.

[3] Arnold et al., *Life at Home in the Twenty-First Century: 32 Families Open Their Doors*, 26.

[4] "Highlights of Annual 2013 Characteristics of New Housing," United States Census Bureau, https://www.census.gov/construction/chars/highlights.html.

Chapter 02: Simplifying

[1] Henry David Thoreau, *Walden*. Public domain.

[2] Arnold et al., *Life at Home in the Twenty-First Century: 32 Families Open Their Doors*, 24.

[3] Kim John Payne, *Simplicity Parenting: Using the Extraordinary Power of Less to Raise Calmer, Happier, and More Secure Kids* (New York: Ballantine Books Trade Paperbacks, 2010), 60.

Chapter 04: Decorating

[1] Patricia Callahan and Sam Roe, "Fear Fans Flames for Chemical Makers," *Chicago Tribune*, May 6, 2012, http://www.chicagotribune.com/news/ct-met-flame-retardants-20120506-story.html#page=1.

[2] "An Introduction to Indoor Air Quality - Volatile Organic Compounds," EPA, http://www.epa.gov/iaq/voc.html#Steps.

Chapter 06: Getting Dressed

[1] Elizabeth Cline, *Overdressed* (New York: Penguin, 2012), 102.

[2] Cline, *Overdressed*, 5.

3   Cline, *Overdressed*, 5.

Chapter 08: Cleaning
1   "Take Out Toxics," Natural Resources Defense Council,
    http://www.nrdc.org/health/toxics.asp

Chapter 09: Thriving
1   "Interior Landscape Plants for Indoor Air Pollution
    Abatement" (report, NASA, September 15, 1989), B.C.
    Wolverton, Anne Johnson, and Keith Bounds, http://ntrs.
    nasa.gov/archive/nasa/casi.ntrs.nasa.gov/19930073077.pdf.

Further Reading:
*Simplicity Parenting: Using the Extraordinary Power of Less
    to Raise Calmer, Happier, and More Secure Kids* by Kim
    John Payne
*Family Herbal: A Guide to Living Life with Energy, Health,
    and Vitality* by Rosemary Gladstar
Herbs for Natural Beauty by Rosemary Gladstar
Make Your Place: Affordable, Sustainable Nesting Skills by
    Raleigh Briggs
*The Home Apothecary: Cold Spring Apothecary's Cookbook of
    Hand-crafted Remedies and Recipes for the Hair, Skin, Body,
    and Home* by Stacey Dugliss-Wesselman
The Naturally Clean Home by Karyn Siegel-Maier
The Omnivore's Dilemma by Michael Pollan
Skin Cleanse by Adina Grigore

For more of my thoughts on simple living, visit my blog,
Reading My Tea Leaves (www.readingmytealeaves.com).

ACKNOWLEDGMENTS

Thanks to Rebecca Kaplan and Holly Dolce, my editors at Abrams Books, who believed in this project and helped breathe life into this book. To Michael Clark, Zachary Knoll, Juliana Horbachevsky, and the rest of the team at Abrams for working so hard on my behalf. And to Jenny Kraemer for turning my words and pictures into these beautiful pages.

To my literary agent, Carla Glasser, for waiting patiently until I was ready and then hustling like a champion. To Jenny Fiedler, Dervla Kelly, Joanna Goddard, and countless other friends for sparking the idea that there might be a book to write in the first place. To the editors at *Remodelista* and *Gardenista*, the *Equals Record*, *Pure Green* magazine, and *Kinfolk* magazine, for giving me the space to hone my craft. And to the faithful readers of my own blog, *Reading My Tea Leaves*, for their support, encouragement, and good cheer.

To Lourdes Uribe for taking such sweet, smart care of my girl while I wrote. And most especially to my family: To my sisters for reading my earliest drafts and lending their wit, sensitivity, and brilliance to the final product. To my mom and dad for offering a lifetime of advice and encouragement in concerns of house and heart. To my husband, James, without whom there would be no story to tell. And to my daughter, Faye, for making it all matter, simply.

Editor: Rebecca Kaplan
Designer: Jenny Kraemer
Production Manager: Anet Sirna-Bruder

Library of Congress Control Number: 2014959568

ISBN: 978-1-4197-1863-2

Copyright © Erin Boyle

Published in 2016 by Abrams Image, an imprint of
ABRAMS. All rights reserved. No portion of this book
may be reproduced, stored in a retrieval system, or
transmitted in any form or by any means, mechanical,
electronic, photocopying, recording, or otherwise,
without written permission from the publisher.

Printed and bound in the United States
10 9 8 7 6 5 4 3 2 1

Abrams Image books are available at special discounts
when purchased in quantity for premiums and promotions
as well as fundraising or educational use. Special editions
can also be created to specification. For details, contact
specialsales@abramsbooks.com or the address below.

115 West 18th Street
New York, NY 10011
www.abramsbooks.com